Contents

Editorial

Bridget Walker

Disaster response has been described as the last resort of the amateur, an unkind assessment but not without a grain of truth. Disaster generates an emotional response and, with each new disaster, new disaster organisations are born, and past lessons on disaster management have to be learned anew.
World Disaster Report 1993 ZFRC and RCS

There is now widespread acceptance that the integration of gender considerations is essential to effective and equitable development programmes. Gender studies are a legitimate area of research; gender analysis and gender training are part of the development agency toolkit; 'gender impact statements' are required in funding proposals, whether to governments or to the international non-governmental development organisations (NGOs). And although the gap between rhetoric and reality is still wide, and practice on the ground falls far short of the ideal, there is some consensus on the goals for which we are striving.

By contrast, the incorporation of gender perspectives in responses to disasters and emergencies is far less developed, and remains relatively unresearched and undocumented. For some funders and operational agencies the integration of gender considerations into relief programmes is an irrelevance, or at best an optional extra, to be bolted on if there is

time, rather than being seen as central to planning and implementation of the relief response. There is often a failure to link emergency and ongoing development programmes. Yet disasters and emergencies are increasingly part of the development agency agenda, as the capacity of poor communities to survive gives way beneath the strain of flood, drought, or conflict, or a combination of crises. An internal report on Oxfam's response to the 1989 Bangladesh floods points out: 'the overall context of relief and development — the social and political environment that people inhabit — is the same. That is the enduring reality after the crisis is past and the programme is complete.'

There are several factors distinguishing disaster response which may lead to a false dichotomy between relief and development, and play a role in marginalising gender considerations. The swift and sudden devastation of earthquakes and floods, the flight of thousands of people seeking refuge from conflict, are highly visible and seen to be obviously life-threatening in a way that the slow and insidious effects of living in continuing poverty are not. Thus disasters soon become public property, through media coverage which focuses on the striking and sensational, and rarely examines the long-term implications or follows the story through. Agencies are faced with the challenge to be seen to be responding, and to be doing so swiftly.

Responding to disasters is expensive and forward budgeting is difficult. Donors often hold emergency funds in different budgets from those for development work, for a range of reasons, including the need to have systems for rapid response which would not be regarded as appropriate for the appraisal of funding proposals for long-term development programmes. It can be difficult to find funding for relief programmes which include developmental components, such as training.

It is not only at the funding level that relief and development programmes are dealt with differently. Implementation of emergency programmes may be the responsibility of a separate department, and contracts for relief workers are often short-term, which means that lessons learned in one emergency are less readily passed on to the new group of people responding to the next disaster. Relief and development work is handled by different sets of actors, from funding through to implementation of the programme, and dialogue between them is often limited.

The context in which most relief programmes are designed and implemented makes the need for a swift response pre-eminent. Complex logistics are involved, requiring co-ordination with a wide range of governmental and non-governmental organisations, and there are often major technical problems of providing emergency shelter, food, and water to large numbers of people who have been displaced. There may be political sensitivities, particularly in responding to the needs of refugee populations. Relief programmes tend to be conceived and delivered in a top-down manner, which precludes discussion with the affected community in general, overlooks gender considerations in particular, and may result in inappropriate responses. Women, especially, lack access to discussions about

their needs, and are rarely involved in planning and policy making. Yet the majority of those affected by emergencies are likely to be women and their children. Even where there is official recognition of gender considerations in emergencies, practice on the ground may fail to take these into account. For example, UNHCR has developed policy and protection guidelines for refugee women, and a set of training materials for use with people engaged in work with refugees. Yet women in refugee camps are still subject to harassment and abuse.

The papers in this issue of Focus on Gender explore some of the dilemmas for those engaged in planning and implementation of emergency relief programmes and record the experience of women in situations of crisis, their particular vulnerabilities and needs, and their capacities and strengths.

A prevailing theme is that of the need to see relief and development as parts of the same whole rather than as different poles. In her article Mary Anderson looks at the factors which create disaster, and suggests an analytical framework of capacities and vulnerabilities in which gender analysis is central. For Deborah Eade and Suzanne Williams there are underlying principles for every programme, whether it is termed relief or development. For Pamela Greet the problem is often in the eye of the beholder. Assumptions must be challenged, perceptions questioned, cultural baggage unpacked, if we are to see through to the realities of what disasters mean for the lives of the women, men and children who experience them.

Understanding gender relations is particularly important in times of disaster, not only because women and children are disproportionately affected, but also because emergency interventions can seriously compromise the long-term future for women by creating further imbalance in their relations with men at a time of stress.

Floods in Bangladesh. A recurring crisis, which people, and the agencies who work with them, have to learn to cope with.   BADAL/OXFAM

It is women who are concerned with the basic necessities of human existence: the provision and preparation of food, the collection of water, the management of the home, keeping both family and homestead clean and in good health. Women, too, are emotional managers — providing security for their children, support to their men. When disaster strikes, women need support in maintaining their reproductive role, but too often, they have been marginalised and undermined. Oxfam's staff team in Darfur wrote ' approaches to emergencies as they stand currently blatantly hand the power over traditional women's affairs to men ... running food distribution, water programmes, blanket, jerrycan and other distributions ... reassigning the traditional women's responsibilities of food and shelter provision to men.'

For many women, the home is the one place where they may exercise some authority. Where the public domain is not open to women, the loss of home is particularly serious. For the Kasaian women forced out of their homes in Shaba in Zaire, and the Indian women rendered homeless by the earthquake in Maharashtra, the pain of bereavement is compounded by the loss of home and lack of private space. The impact of over-crowding has a direct effect on their ability to cope. The Zairean women fear the effect on their adolescent children, who, by leaving the cramped conditions of the family shelter are likely to become vulnerable, and find the only means of support will be on the streets, through petty crime and prostitution. Women's responsibility for childcare and the support they require in times of disaster need to be further explored.

It is important to understand how disaster affects women not just in their reproductive roles but also in their roles as producers and providers. In many of the case studies women refer to their loss of earning capacity and their worries about unemployment and lack of income. The particular difficulties for women managing their households without male support are highlighted in the experiences of drought in southern Africa. Wilfrid Tichagwa emphasises the need to strengthen women as farmers in their own right. Disaster responses may include employment opportunities — women as well as men should be able to benefit from these, both immediately and in the long term.

In a crisis, needs may seem to be at their most basic and immediate. Yet women themselves retain a long-term view which those seeking to support them would do well to heed. In Zaire and in India, women expressed their concern that their children were out of school. Eileen Maybin, in her article on the Maharashtra earthquake, points out how important it is not to lose sight, in the immediate pressure to respond to practical needs, of women's long-term and strategic interests, and the particular difficulties they experience because of their subordinate position. There is a sad contradiction between the generous assistance offered to the earthquake survivors and the predatory approach to women who have lost the protection of male relatives.

Breakdown in social cohesion can lead to serious threats to women's safety and security. Violence against women, rape and sexual harassment are present in every crisis — not just as weapons of war and armed conflict. Technical programmes have a social impact; the design of shelter, siting of water and sanitation facilities, accommodating of widows and women on their own can all either support women or increase their vulnerability.

In his article on the Rohingya refugees Gawher Nayeem Wahra describes how women who have suffered abuse may not receive sympathetic treatment. In emergencies, women's health needs — medical care for injuries they have sustained, or treatment for sexually transmitted disease — may not be met. In refugee situations family planning may be regarded as a luxury, and unwanted pregnancy an issue over which there is a conspiracy of silence. Health guides draw attention to the needs of pregnant women and nursing mothers; the Bangladesh cyclone of 1991 highlighted the needs of another group, women who had lost the babies they had been breastfeeding. It is only recently that more attention has been given to the needs of women who are menstruating or experiencing disturbances to the menstrual cycle. There is now some awareness of the psychosocial effects of disaster but there is still much to be done to incorporate an understanding of these and an appropriate response into relief programmes. Women's supportive social networks are likely to be impaired in times of disaster and social dislocation, and as in the Maharashtra earthquake, the circumstances of relief assistance and temporary shelter make it difficult for such networks to be used effectively.

The hardships which women suffer, both as members of a community in crisis and as women within that community, must be recognised and addressed. However, another predominant theme in the papers is the emphasis on women as survivors. Crisis also creates opportunity. This is illustrated in the programmes to address drought in Zambia, and in the involvement of Saharawi women in every aspect of the organisation of their refugee camps. Seeing people as a resource rather than a burden, looking at their skills and strengths as well as their needs and vulnerabilities, must be part of the aid response.

The primary task is still to learn how to listen to women, and translate understanding into positive action. This is likely to be most effective where there are organisations already in place which are gender sensitive. Their response to disaster will consciously seek to include women in their plans, although this may not be easy. Ideally, women should be involved in carrying out surveys and assessments of emergency situations, but local agencies cannot easily mobilise women in emergencies, and may be reluctant to send women workers into an unknown situation. But women's experiences must be made known, and the case studies from Pakistan and India illustrate the limitations of relief responses which have not taken gender issues into account.

Where disaster-preparedness plans exist they should be gender aware. Mary Myers suggests how plans drawn up at national level can be made more gender sensitive in advance of a crisis. The development-emergency link is made in the case studies from Kenya, Uganda and Zambia. In Kenya, food distribution mechanisms were informed by long-term knowledge of the coping strategies of the Turkana, and were designed to preserve these cultural practices and to support women in their role of food providers. In Uganda, women were actively involved in the design and maintenance of an emergency water project. This called for skills which they had acquired in their home country; an illustration of the importance of training for women in both emergency and normal situations. It is clear, too, that the skills which the Sahrawi women have learned in exile will stand them in good stead.

In Zambia, the relationships built up with communities during a long-term development programme were important in enabling a drought response where relief and recovery programmes were consciously designed as part of a grassroots democratisation process in which both women and men had an important role to play.

Disasters are times of extremes of human experience. They put communities under the microscope and reveal their complexities, their relationships with the environment, their structures of power. These papers show how action in emergencies holds the potential for deepening existing inequalities or for positive use of the conditions which have been created for catalytic change. They argue that an understanding of gender relations is fundamental to effective disaster responses; the litmus test for evaluating an emergency programme is whether women's position has been diminished or enhanced. Women facing the collapse of their lives describe their harrowing experiences, and their continuing struggle to supply the basic needs for themselves and their families and the lack of opportunities and rights which limit their capacity. Their stories also illustrate their resourcefulness and strength, and ability to organise in the midst of disintegration — the groundrock on which to build future livelihoods which are just and sustainable.

Even in the most adverse situations, people demonstrate resourcefulness and self–reliance. Sowing beans, on a small plot of ground in a refugee camp in Uganda (see article by Joy Morgan in this issue).   Joy Morgan/Oxfam

Understanding the disaster-development continuum
Gender analysis is the essential tool

Mary B Anderson

Increasingly, the agencies of the United Nations, the development bureaux of donor nations, and the large number of non-governmental organisations (NGOs) that work in countries striving to achieve development are focusing their attention on understanding the relationships between disasters and development. This focus is motivated by two recent trends. First, the number of disasters worldwide is rising, with an increasing number of people suffering as a result. Recognising this situation, aid workers are expressing growing frustration that they continue to respond only to symptoms rather than addressing the causes of disasters. Second, a reduction in overall aid budgets is apparent in many donor countries today, with an accompanying shift of these shrinking funds away from development programmes and towards disaster response. As a result, both development and relief workers are seeking ways to use available relief funds to meet the emergency needs of disaster victims and, at the same time, support fundamental change towards long-term development.

These two motivations — an urgent need to deal with the causes of disasters rather than only with the symptoms, and the necessity of getting the best possible short-term and long-term outcomes from aid funds — are forcing a harder look at the tools that are available for effective planning and programming. One such tool, which can contribute significantly to addressing root causes and which can support effective, efficient and equitable long-term development, is gender analysis.

Causes rather than symptoms

When considering the causes of a disaster, the basic question is: What makes disasters happen? It is now widely acknowledged that disasters occur as a result of human actions and human decisions, rather than as 'acts of God'. A strong wind at sea that does no damage to human life or property does not represent a disaster, whereas if that same wind comes on shore where people have built flimsy homes in vulnerable locations it will create a disaster. An earthquake can cause massive death and damage when buildings are weak and preparations inadequate, but another earthquake of the same force can cause little or no damage where building technologies have been developed to withstand tremors and building codes adopted and enforced to ensure that these technologies are used. Increasing flooding occurs downstream from deforested areas or where silting has occurred as a result of erosion. Human agency plays a role in whether or not these natural phenomena — winds, earth movements and rains — do or do not become disasters. The centrality of human actions and choices in causing disasters is even more obvious in the growing number of 'complex' emergencies — that is, those disasters that involve both environmental elements and civil conflict.

Because disasters are not brought about solely by natural causes, their impacts are not random. Some individuals and groups become victims while others remain relatively unscathed. The first step in under-

Because disasters are not brought about solely by natural causes, their impacts are not random.

standing and preparing to deal with root causes is to analyse why some people are vulnerable to disasters and others are not.

Vulnerability to disasters can be analysed in three categories.[1] First, people may be physically vulnerable. They may live in poorly-built houses on land that is susceptible to catastrophe; they may be poor and have few reserves and no insurance to aid recovery if some crisis occurs. Second, people may be socially vulnerable by being marginalised and excluded from decision-making and political processes. Third, people may be psychologically vulnerable if they feel powerless, victimised, and unable to take effective actions for their own security.

How does gender analysis help us understand vulnerability? Gender is certainly not the only determining factor of vulnerability, nor is it always the most important. However, very often an understanding of vulnerability and the development of strategies for overcoming it can be advanced through gender analysis.

It is often said that 'women are among the most vulnerable'. Why is this so? Women are also strong and capable. They manage and sustain families under the most deplorable conditions. They are producers of a range of goods and services on which the survival of their societies depends. What makes them vulnerable?

In general, around the world, women are poorer than men. Their poverty arises from the roles they are assigned and the limits placed by societies on their access to and control of resources. Women are disproportionately employed in unpaid, underpaid and non-formal sectors of economies. Inheritance laws and traditions, marriage arrangements, banking systems and social patterns that reinforce women's dependence on fathers, husbands and sons all contribute both to their unfavourable access to resources and their lack of power to change things. The health dangers that result from multiple births can contribute to interrupted work and low productivity. Traditional expectations and home-based responsibilities that limit women's mobility also limit their opportunities for political involvement, education, access to information, markets, and a myriad of other resources, the lack of which reinforces the cycle of their vulnerability.

Understanding these linkages through gender analysis makes it clear that women are vulnerable not because it is in their physical nature to be weak but because of the arrangements of societies that result in their poverty, political marginalisation, and dependence on men. As the number of households that are headed by women increases, worldwide, these causes of vulnerability have broader implications for the dependents in such families.

Furthermore, understanding that vulnerability is a condition caused by human actions and attitudes can provide insights about strategies for addressing vulnerability and thus dealing with the causes, rather than symptoms, of disasters. Poverty-reduction strategies should have as one major focus the reduction of poverty among women and, particularly, among female-headed households. Such efforts must be designed with attention to the educational, locational, time and tradition-based constraints that women encounter.

Gender analysis can also aid the identification of circumstances in which men may be vulnerable. An example of this comes from a refugee camp in Western Ethiopia where many young Sudanese men were gathered who, having walked long distances to escape conscription into armies, were in exceedingly poor health. Food was immediately shipped into this camp in quantities considered adequate to rebuild their health, but morbidity and mortality rates remained high. Investigation showed that these male refugees were continuing to starve because the food they were given needed to be cooked before it could be eaten, and their gendered roles had precluded their ever learning about food preparation.

Linking short-term help to long-term outcomes

The second issue faced by aid workers today is the necessity of ensuring that short-term, relief assistance both meets immediate needs of disaster victims and, at the same time, supports their achievement of long-term developmental goals. Too often, relief assistance has increased the dependency of recipients on continuing aid rather than enabled them to move forward toward self-sufficiency. For example, it is now widely recognised that an influx of donated food, deemed necessary for saving people from starvation, can also undermine market prices and, therefore, the incentives of local farmers to plant the next season's crop. Thus, relief aid can contribute to future and spiralling disaster conditions. Less recognised, but also well-documented, is the long-term negative effect on relief recipients of the organisational systems for distributing goods or prioritising needs that are imposed by donors in their anxiety to meet urgent emergency needs efficiently. Approaches

that deny andundermine the existing physical and organisational capacities of recipient groups also undermine and weaken their subsequent abilities to plan, manage and achieve independent self-sufficiency.

Again, gender analysis provides one critical tool for understanding the linkages between short-term aid and long-term outcomes. If it is critical, when providing emergency assistance, to work with rather than for disaster victims in order to ensure positive long-term impacts, then it is equally critical to identify the capacities of the recipients concerned, because it is these capacities that must be supported if long-term development is to be achieved. The gender roles ascribed to men and women mean that they have different physical, social and psychological capacities in any given context. The scarcity of aid resources makes it even more important to target and tailor assistance to fit local realities.

To return to the situation described above, when aid workers identified the cause of continuing hunger among the young Sudanese men in the Ethiopian refugee camp, they were able to organise the ten per cent of the population who were women with cooking skills, to teach the men how to cook. Recognition of and support for existing capacities associated with gendered roles may make the difference between a programme's effectiveness or failure. For example, efforts to arrange water supplies for disaster victims and development project participants alike have, often, succeeded or foundered depending on whether they took account of women's involvement in water collection and usage, and whether they supported, or failed to support, women's capacities to manage and maintain water pumps and other equipment. Similarly, experience has provided too many examples of programmes that have issued drought-resistant seeds and provided technical assistance about new

The task of providing water for family needs becomes very arduous in times of drought. Programmes to supply water for people affected by drought need to take account of women's involvement in water collection and usage.   JULIAN QUAN/OXFAM

farming methods to male members of disaster-affected groups, to enable families to replant and increase food production; but, because women have been primarily responsible for household food production, these technologies have not been adopted.

In all societies, men and women experience different vulnerabilities and have different capacities as a result of their gendered roles. Sometimes these roles are very different and rigid; sometimes they are overlapping and fluid. In either case, the failure to identify gendered roles and to plan programmes with them consciously in mind has resulted in the inequitable delivery of disaster relief assistance, and inadequate attention to the potential long-term outcomes of short-term interventions. The tool of gender analysis is a powerful one for accurately diagnosing opportunities and constraints in any programme

situation, and for identifying more effective strategies for delivering emergency assistance so that it supports long-term development for women and men, and girls and boys.

[1] This understanding of the three categories of vulnerabilities and capacities, discussed later, were developed through a broadly-based collaborative effort of NGOs and other donor agencies called the International Relief/Development Project. Its fuller results are available in: Anderson, Mary B. and Peter J. Woodrow, *Rising from the Ashes: Development Strategies at Times of Disaster*, 1989, Westview and UNESCO Presses, Boulder and Paris.

Mary B Anderson is President of Collaborative Development Action Inc., Cambridge, Mass.

Making good policy into good practice

Pamela Greet

What is *Who is speaking*

What is shown *Who is interested*

What is observed *Who is interested*

What is overlooked *Who is silent*

What is not said *Who is silent*

What is explained *Who is present*

What is recorded *Who is listening*

What is forgotten *Who is deceived*

What is assumed *Who is trusted*

What is hidden *Who is present*

What is sensed *Who is frightened*

What is ignored *Who is asking*

What is misunderstood *Who is attentive*

What is not seen *Who is forgotten*

What is not explained *Who is watching*

What is not heard *Who is involved*

What is not asked *Who is silent?*

Women are everywhere *and are also silent and invisible.*

I wrote this piece last year after a week of intense field visits throughout drought-stricken Mozambique. During this week I was impressed by the invisibility and muteness of women. Time and again we flew into remote rural stations (myself — one woman with male counterparts from our implementing partners), to be greeted and briefed on the impact of the drought by local NGOs and government officials (mostly male); drove into settlements where local headmen and community leaders (all male) told us what their needs were; and spoke with representative heads of families (usually male) who related their experience.

Meanwhile around us women were carrying out their normal daily activities which kept the families alive: carrying heavy bundles of fuelwood; queuing for water, carrying water; searching for food (many families survived the harshest times by eating things collected from the forests); tending kitchen gardens; preparing food.

From what I could see, women were bearing the strongest impact of the drought: it was their lives and their work which were cruelly changed, yet only men were brought forward to relate this to us.

On one occasion, in an area from which I knew many men had left to work in the mines in South Africa, I asked the local official about the number of female-headed households. He responded that there were some but 'not many'. This was in a place where an extensive shanty-town had grown up on the edge of the town, and unofficial reports indicated that women were being physically endangered whilst fetching water and firewood. I asked were women not facing additional problems because they had to travel longer distances, often getting up at 3 or 4 a.m., to fetch water from distances of up to 15 kilometres. 'No', I was told. 'In fact it may be easier for women now because they are given food rations, preparing their family's meals is simpler.'

These experiences led me to reflect on how we see things when we make visits to affected communities. What is the reality of the situation on the ground and what is the picture we form of it and communicate to others? We often find it difficult in such situations to speak to women or to hear their concerns, especially when men are the responsible local authorities, men are our guides and interpreters.

We each carry with us our own assumptions and prejudices, our own agenda, our own pressure and concerns. As much as what we see, these are the influences that shape our observations and our thoughts. When we communicate (in informal and formal discussions, in meetings and conversations) and when we observe (in villages and offices), what we see and how we interpret what we see can be as much a product of this personal and cultural baggage as what is there in front of us. We need to question ourselves and to be always aware of how we perceive our world. Are women at the centre of our mental picture, or are they in the shadows, silently carrying out their everyday work?

Putting women centre stage

There has been enough lip-service paid to the importance of providing more effectively for women. Most of the major emergency-response organisations (UN and large NGOs) can point to policy papers and guidelines which spell out what the organisation strives to do in relation to women. But we have to challenge ourselves on how well these policies are carried out in practice. In many cases the re-occurrence of emergencies or crises demonstrates the failure of the development strategies in which we have been engaged. Part of this

failure has been the result of marginalising women's needs and women's role in production and development. Women's concerns, women's programmes and initiatives remain marginal almost 20 years after the 1975 Nairobi launch of the Decade for Women because we have failed to recognise the central role played by women in most of the communities and societies we are trying to help.

In the following paragraphs some suggestions are outlined for ways to redress this situation.

Gender awareness

There is a gender dimension to all crisis situations and to our actions and responses. In emergency situations the need for quick action may be used as an excuse for ignoring the gender dimensions of the needs and our responses, and for precluding proper consultation, the key to effective planning and delivery.

The notion of gender awareness challenges each of us at a very personal (and confronting) level, to examine our own responses and perceptions of women: if we are to consult them we must believe they have something important to say.

Emergency responses almost always seem to focus on the negative aspects: the destruction, the suffering, and the needs. A proper assessment of the 'damage' is central to an effective response, but what is there to build on? What elements of the community have survived that our response can facilitate and enhance in a process in which the relief phase should be seen as a first step to recovery and further growth and development?

From this perspective we understand the need to identify the ways in which communities cope. Is there a positive image that emerges from the crisis? It is incumbent on us not just to refer to this in the images portrayed in communications to the public through the mass media (awareness and fund-raising or promotional materials) but also in the images and messages portrayed through the language of programme proposals and documentation. Attention should be given to the strengths of the community so that programmes enhance these rather than create further dependency. Gender awareness is central to this approach. Women are generally the chief providers of food and emotional security in most family situations. When an emergency occurs, they not only have to cope with their own physical and emotional reaction to the crisis but also to support their family in both physical and psychological terms. Women are often the greatest strength a community has. Our approach should highlight these strengths rather than undermining them, as would many traditional 'quick response' programmes.

Women's needs must be taken into account, remembering that they carry this double burden. In most crises (especially conflict-related, mass displacement and refugee situations) women and dependent children make up the majority of those affected. Yet, women are generally precluded from discussions about their needs and are still only rarely consulted in planning or decision making. It is therefore essential to find ways of working with women. Awareness of their needs is not enough. It must be backed up by policy, and policy must be translated into implementation. Implementation must be monitored, evaluated and revised in a continuous process of improving our ways of working.

Assessment and planning

To address properly the needs in any given situation it is important to have an informed picture of the affected populations. Proper demographic information, disaggregated for sex and age, can assist in addressing health, security and other specific areas for action in a gender-sensitive way. It may require a special effort to find out how women have been affected by the emergency, what their needs and concerns are, and to involve them in decision-making at the planning stage.

Delivery of assistance

Once a clear picture can be drawn of the impact of the situation, it is possible to provide assistance in a way which is sensitive to women's needs and which will, at least, not make their normal everyday tasks more difficult. They should be consulted about all decisions regarding distribution of food, water and other items. Make women key players in evaluation and assessment processes, which should be on-going throughout the programme.

Training

Training and effective staff development policies should focus on strategies to bring more women into decision-making positions in relief and development organisations. Recruitment of women is only partly a solution. For too long it has been perceived as women's responsibility to ensure that women's needs are addressed and met. Through gender-awareness training our male colleagues can be encouraged to see how attention to gender issues will ultimately strengthen programmes and make them more effective in reaching their targets and fulfilling the communities' needs.

Training is needed at all levels to develop awareness of gender issues in emergencies. We have to take responsibility for challenging within our own organisations, with partners and co-operating bodies such as governments, donors and UN systems, how well policy is put into practice and what resources are committed for training to ensure that policy is translated into practice.

Pamela Greet is Consultant to the Emergencies Desk at the World Council of Churches in Geneva.

'Women and children first'

Introducing a gender strategy into disaster preparedness

Mary Myers

The scope of disaster management is wide; it embraces decisions made at all levels, from central government to the grass-roots. Plans for disaster preparedness, however, tend not to be made on the ground, they are made in capital cities by government ministries. Such plans normally begin with a national disaster-preparedness plan.

In many disaster-prone countries of the South, a national disaster plan is often inherited, or copied directly, from the former colonial power. Increasingly, though, governments are improving and updating their plans. Often this is being done in the light of lessons painfully learned in the aftermath of disasters of horrendous proportions.

Gender is an issue which tends to have a low profile in national disaster plans. In contrast to development, where gender considerations have become almost obligatory for planners, in the area of disasters they are still seen as somewhat of a 'luxury'. Particularly in rapid-onset disasters, the received idea is that gender issues must be put 'on hold' for the duration of an emergency. Planners at central government level, most of whom are men, will perhaps consider women's needs and position after a disaster strikes, but certainly not 'in the heat of the moment'. In effect, when it comes to disaster preparedness, the old maxim 'Women and Children First', turns out in practice to be the exact opposite.

How, then, to introduce the idea of gender into disaster preparedness strategy? More specifically, how best to insert gender issues into a country's national disaster plan? The United Nations is currently carrying out a series of disaster management training seminars in which middle to high-ranking government officials are invited to discuss and improve their disaster plans. One of the UN manuals (UNDP/UNDRO 1992) sets out a useful framework upon which a national disaster preparedness strategy can be developed. The manual recommends nine inter-related components:

1 Vulnerability assessment
2 Planning
3 Institutional framework
4 Information systems
5 Resource base
6 Warning systems
7 Response mechanisms
8 Public education and training
9 Rehearsals

These components could be used as 'pegs' on which to hang discussion of gender issues. The following are a few suggestions for provoking discussion and action.

Manab Mukti Songstha (MMS) is an NGO in Bangladesh which supports groups working on disaster–preparedness. Some groups have set up disaster funds, to buy food and medicine, to which every member contributes. These houses have been raised above flood level by communal labour.

CLARE HANTON-KHAN/OXFAM

1 Vulnerability assessment

In your risk-mapping, have you disaggregated the vulnerable population by sex? What do the results show? Have you considered in what ways women might form an especially vulnerable group within the high-risk communities you have identified?

2 Planning

In formulating your national disaster plan, have you consulted women at every stage? How is the plan worded? Does it assume that disaster planners are only men, or include women too?

3 Institutional framework

At central government level, has, for example, the ministry responsible for women's affairs been included in the coordination plan? At community level, are women represented on local committees?

4 Information systems (in order to predict forthcoming emergencies)

In your data-collection plans, have indicators based on women's needs and coping strategies been taken into account? In other words, how have you ensured that you listen to women at the grassroots?

5 Resource base

Have your stocks been planned with women's needs in mind (eg. Do your medical supplies include obstetric/gynaecological medicines/equipment? Do your supplementary food-stocks correspond with local cooking customs?) Are you assuming that women and children are just victims, or have you planned your resource base to build on their strengths? Have your resources been planned with a long-term reconstruction and recovery phase in mind?

6 *Warning systems*

In giving a vulnerable population notice of an impending disaster, are you using appropriate media to ensure you are reaching all sectors of the population, especially women and children? (Remember that more women than men are non-literate and tend only to speak their mother tongue.)

7 *Response mechanisms*

Are all the mechanisms you plan to put in place sensitive to women's needs and abilities? How will you ensure that 'in the heat of the moment' women will not be sidelined and rendered even more vulnerable? What are your plans to encourage women survivors in the disaster relief process? On the other hand, is there a danger that your relief plans will overburden women as carers and thereby create unforeseen problems further down the line? How have you anticipated the gender dynamics/conflicts that will inevitably be brought on by trauma?

8 *Public education and training*

Have women been included and appropriately targeted by educational campaigns designed to prepare populations for disasters? Are women's talents as informal educators being tapped? Have women's heavy domestic workloads been taken into account when designing training schemes?

9 *Rehearsals*

How are you ensuring that women (as well as children and the elderly) are taking part in rehearsals? Are your drills planned with women's domestic timetables in mind? Do they take account of and realistically simulate cultural norms within society?

These suggestions are basically a checklist, and are therefore somewhat dry. They could be supplemented, as the occasion demanded, by appropriate 'real life' examples, and given different emphases according to the hazard(s) in question. By giving gender issues a practical focus in this way, it should be possible to influence planners' thinking at an early stage in the disaster cycle. If women are taken into account at the preparation stage, it should be easier for planners to integrate gender issues into the emergency response phase, and so-on towards long-term development.

Perhaps more than any other, the gender issue brings into sharp focus the importance of making the relief-development link. The current tendency to ignore gender issues in disasters feeds into the false idea that there should be a gap between relief and development. By integrating gender issues into their national disaster plan, planners could come significantly closer to a result which some might find surprising: that is, a change in the inbuilt inequalities and gender imbalances in society which have for so long put a brake on sustainable development.

Reference

UNDP/UNDRO (1992) *An Overview of Disaster Management*, training module for use in the United Nations Disaster Management Training Programme.

Mary Myers is a Programme Director at the Cranfield Disaster Preparedness Centre. She is currently involved in coordinating a series of workshops in Francophone Africa with the United Nations Disaster Management Training Programme.

Emergencies and development

Ageing with wisdom and dignity

Deborah Eade and Suzanne Williams

Many of the international NGOs which were born in the 1940s are currently facing a mid-life crisis. They started out under the humanitarian mandate of relieving civilian suffering and saving lives. They came of age in the 1960s, and discovered 'development' during a period of fervent intellectual experimentation and iconoclasm, not only in Europe and North America, but also in what came to be called 'developing countries', as these struggled to free themselves from the legacies of colonialism. Development studies provided a theoretical basis for the activities of NGOs, just as national liberation struggles became the arena for their practical involvement.[1] It rapidly became clear that prevention is better than cure: that pre-emptive development is better than after-the-event emergency relief.

In time, the emphasis on providing grants for projects gave way to a deeper appreciation of the *processes* of social, political, economic, and cultural change. Within the NGO world, advocacy — in the form of public opinion-forming, political lobbying, focused campaigning, and development education — was increasingly seen as a vital component of social transformation. Feminism also provided insights into the differentiated impact of NGO development and relief interventions on women, men and children. The feminist critique maintained that many well-intentioned efforts had either ignored women (and children) altogether, or had tended to worsen their condition, both in absolute terms and relative to men. Accordingly, during the 1980s, most major NGOs made some attempt to incorporate an awareness of gender-based injustice in their development, relief and advocacy work. For example, Mary Anderson and others[2] designed frameworks, to be used in the official and the NGO sector, for basing emergency relief on the principles of development by ensuring that it is administered in such a way as to identify and strengthen the existing capacities of women and men, while at the same time working to reduce those areas in which they are, or may become, vulnerable. The gender dimensions of power, in terms of access to and control of resources, were central to this way of looking at the working practice of relief agencies.

From this perspective, emergency relief was not just about efficient logistics, rapid delivery systems, and articulate political lobbying, crucial though these might be in mounting an effective aid programme. It was, just as much as long-term development, about enhancing the *quality* of people's lives: raising the level of what women, men and children are (and feel) entitled to demand, both for themselves and for future generations; listening sensitively to what people have to say, even if their views are not always what aid agencies want (or expect) to hear; and seeing that the concerns and perspectives of women and men are represented in the decision-making (including planning and evaluation) processes which are relevant to them. After half-a-century of experience, what NGOs had come to realise was that development and relief efforts which are not good for women and children, as well as for men, are not good.

The active promotion of human rights is central to development and relief work.

However, the international NGO community now enters middle age in a gloomier ideological climate, and in a world which worships at the shrine of the market-place, and measures success in terms of quantitative targets. (How much money can we raise? How many projects can we fund? Are we beating our rivals?) A world which appears to value speed, photo opportunities, and the high-impact drama of relief, rather than the slower — but less photogenic — processes of development.

The trouble is that development and relief NGOs have learnt to stand for values which are the antithesis of cut-throat competition — namely, co-operation, collaboration and international solidarity. They are not concerned with growth *per se*; their purpose is social and economic justice for every human being. Their role is not to ensure their own survival at any price, but to work for alternatives to the ruthless logic of the market. However, these core values tend to get left behind in the rush to be bigger and faster than everyone else.

Below are eight basic principles for development and relief work.[3] Rather than

seeing these as two different kinds of interventions, NGOs should redouble their commitment to the lessons of 50 years' experience, in all their work. To aim at anything less is to fail the women, men, and children whose lives are affected by their interventions.

1 **People-centredness:** Development and relief work is about improving the lives of women, men and children. Interventions must *always* be measured in terms of how they affect people's lives, in ways which are meaningful to the people concerned.

2 **Human rights:** The active promotion of human rights is central to development and relief work. These rights include the civil, political, economic, social and cultural rights — individual and collective, personal and public — of all women, men and children.

3 **Empowerment:** Gaining the strength, confidence and vision to work for positive changes in their lives, individually and together with others, is the process of empowerment. Women and men become empowered by their own efforts, not by what others do for them. When development and relief programmes are not firmly based on people's own efforts to work for change, their impact may be *disempowering*.

4 **Participation:** Effective participation means people's right to shape decisions which affect their lives. Women and men are disempowered when they cannot exercise this right. Development and relief work should strengthen people's capacity to participate positively in social change, in terms both of personal growth and public action.

5 **Interdependence:** Societies depend on the inter-relations between women, men, and children, whose needs are distinct, and vary according to cultural, political and economic factors. Development and relief

interventions cannot isolate or 'target' one set of people without also having an impact on the lives and well-being of everyone who relates to them.

6 Change: Development and relief work takes place within a context of wider processes of social change, which are drawn on a far broader canvas than that of NGO interventions. Such processes are messy: social change does not have a clear beginning, middle or end, nor is it predictable or evenly-paced. Social change is almost always differentiated by gender. To be a positive force, NGOs must understand, and be committed to, the processes of change in which they choose to intervene.

7 Sustainability: To be sustainable, the processes of change must promote equity between, and for, all women and men; and enhance their ability to gain a decent living, both now and in the future. Sustainability is more than a matter of financial self-reliance: it depends on people's social and economic capacity to withstand and surmount pressures on their lives, and ways of life.

8 Risk: Development and relief are not risk-free. Women and men take risks when they try to change their lives, and to shape the decisions and processes affecting them. They cannot be certain about the outcomes of their efforts. Likewise, NGOs cannot demand certain returns from the support that they give.

Anxious narcissism is common amongst people who want to conceal their advancing years. Middle-aged NGOs concerned about their profiles should examine their reflections in a complex world and ask whether they really do need a face lift — or whether they should accept their grey hairs with dignity and prize their wrinkles for the wisdom these represent.

Notes

1 The emergence of development studies has not been met with uncritical acceptance by the NGO community. For instance, Michael Edwards, of Save the Children (UK), writes that 'there is sometimes a tendency for people to use these new relationships between research and practice for what are essentially selfish ends. There is a danger that NGOs and development projects will become an *object* for academic study, in much the same way as poor people themselves were treated as objects in the conventional approach to development studies ... to work *together* in a joint search for better practice and better theory ... requires an acceptance of each other as equals', 'Knowledge and action: hope for the future', in Frans J Schuurman (ed) (1993), *Beyond the Impasse: New Directions in Development Theory*, Zed, London, pp 88-89.

2 Mary B Anderson and Peter J Woodrow, (1989) *Rising from the Ashes: Development Strategies in Times of Disaster*, Westview Press Inc, Colorado, and Unesco, Paris.

3 These are based on material prepared by Deborah Eade and Suzanne Williams for the *Oxfam Handbook for Development and Relief*, Oxford (forthcoming, 1994).

Deborah Eade currently edits the journal *Development in Practice*. She has been involved in NGO work since 1979, and was Oxfam's Deputy Regional Representative in Mexico and Central America from 1982-90.

Suzanne Williams founded Oxfam's Gender and Development Unit and is author of the forthcoming *Oxfam Gender Training Manual*. As a social anthropologist, she has 16 years' experience in NGO work, including 4 years as Oxfam's Deputy Country Representative in Brazil, and a number of consultancies on human rights and development work.

Deborah Eade and Suzanne Williams are co-editors of the forthcoming *Oxfam Handbook for Development and Relief*, due to be published in 1994.

The effects of drought on the condition of women

Wilfred Tichagwa

This paper looks at the real or potential impacts of drought on the material conditions of life as they affect rural women. The rationale for focusing on rural women is two-fold. First, rural women are the backbone of the rural economy. Any changes in the condition of women which will affect their performance in economic activities will inevitably affect the performance of the rural economy as a whole. The second point is that at household level, women are to a large extent responsible for food provision and the overall survival strategy of the family. The effects of drought are therefore important to the extent that they undermine the women's efforts to fend for their families.

The following discussion focuses on the economic, environmental, social and health impacts of drought on women.

Economic impacts

As shown in Figure 1, crop failures caused by drought result in food deficits in terms of the household's needs. Also there will be little or no crop surplus for sale, therefore income from this source is reduced or even wiped out completely. It will not be possible therefore for women to buy food when stocks are depleted.

A further possible consequence is increased male labour migration. The women remaining at home end up with an increased number of tasks as they must now do the work for which the migrant males were responsible. Where the men stay away for extended periods, the increased burden of women could result in reduced agricultural productivity. Figure 1 shows that this could lead to vicious circles in which reduced productivity leads to food deficits and reduced income from the sale of reduced surpluses. This in turn could lead to a reinforcement of the male labour migration as part of the solution to the household's needs for food and cash income.

The right-hand part of Figure 1 shows another effect of drought on agricultural production. Depletion of pastures leads to high mortality of cattle. The resultant reduction in draught power means that women have to till the fields by hand, which is back-breaking work; and women are often forced to reduce the area they cultivate.

At national level, the traditional response to drought is the food-for-work or money-for-work programme. Often, the food-for-work projects rely mostly on women's labour because women are seen as the providers of food. Men tend to prefer money-for-work projects as these are seen as substitutes for paid employment, traditionally regarded as men's area. Drought-relief programmes thus tend to

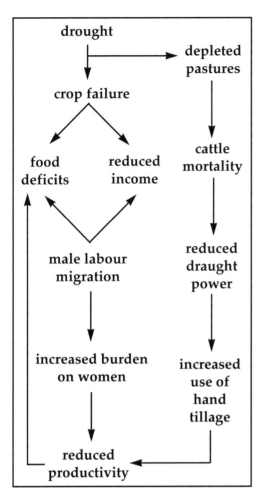

Figure 1: Effects of drought on women's agricultural production and marketing

reinforce the traditional division of labour which places on women a heavy responsibility for reproductive work.

Finally, it is obvious that hunger and malnutrition will leave people in a weak physical condition. There will therefore be a drop in productivity until the nutrition status of the labour force is restored to previous levels. Child labour, in particular, will be greatly reduced. Since children's work is usually undertaken as a helping hand to mothers, then the weaker the children, the more work their mothers must take back from the children. Such tasks as fetching firewood, washing dishes, fetching water, cleaning the house and yard, laundry, gardening, food preparation, and child minding, will all have to be done by the mothers on their own. This, in turn, will have adverse effects on agricultural production.

Environmental impacts

In Figure 2 it can be seen that in some instances women will resort to desperate measures to avert the crisis of hunger in the family. For example, gold-panning in river banks is on the increase in many rural areas. Also the collection of wild fruit and

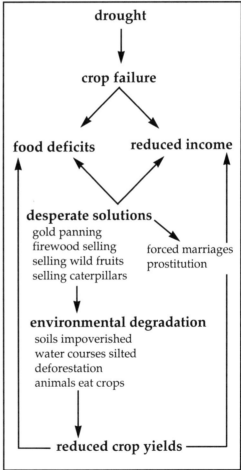

Figure 2: Environmental and social consequences of drought

caterpillars for eating and selling has increased in the last decade. These activities have enabled families to supplement their diets in times of drought. However, they can be dangerous, as when holes dug into river banks cave in and entomb gold-panners; and they can create environmental problems, such as the extensive silting of water courses resulting from indiscriminate gold-panning.

In Matebeleland South, collection of caterpillars has escalated as a consequence not only of recurrent drought but also of the commercial processing and packaging of caterpillars by some big food companies. Villagers have been felling trees for easy access to the caterpillars. The Monpani tree on which caterpillars are found is a slow-growing hardwood, therefore regeneration will take decades. The excessive harvesting of caterpillars threatens them with extinction.

The collection of wild fruit for sale is also reaching alarming proportions. In the area around Domboshawa, the writer witnessed the felling of trees so that fruit could be collected. The fruits were not ripe and therefore could not be shaken down from the high branches, and as the tree has a weak bark and a rather brittle trunk, it is unsafe to climb. The solution is to cut the tree down. As a result, this fruit tree is becoming extinct in some areas.

A group of women were lamenting the likely consequences of tree felling to collect unripe fruits. Firstly, there will be less fruit the following year. Secondly, harvesting both ripe and unripe fruit leaves nothing for the baboons and monkeys to eat, at a time when farmers are planting maize seed. As the animals are capable of uncovering and eating a large proportion of the maize seed, there was a fear that this will result in very low germination rates and reduced crop yields.

Tree felling for firewood for hungry people to sell is also a serious threat to the environment, and has resulted in extensive

Collecting wild fruit: a drought–survival strategy which can have serious environmental consequences.

BAZ SOLANKI/OXFAM

deforestation in some communal areas and resettlement areas. Denuding the land of trees makes it extremely vulnerable to erosion and gully formation.

These desperate solutions to the problem of recurrent food deficits will result in environmental degradation so that in future women will have great difficulty in finding firewood, and timber for building purposes. Denuding the land of its forest cover will result in impoverished soils and consequently poor crop yields. Excessive tree-felling could result in reduced evapo-transpiration, a vital element in the water cycle.

Social impacts

Recurrent drought has in many instances resulted in increased labour migration. In the rural areas, many households are now female-headed. Where the migrant husbands do not remit cash regularly, the wives have a difficult time trying to run the affairs of the household.

In some cases, the trappings of city/town life have turned the otherwise seasonal migrant workers into permanent urban dwellers, with a second wife or more in their second homes. A husband in town may even require his wife in the rural areas to send food to him and his other wife after the harvest, and this practice increases in drought periods.

Another unpleasant consequence of chronic food deficits has been forced marriages for girls so that their parents can survive on the *lobola* (bride-price) paid by her husband. Wives of relatively prosperous men face the danger of finding themselves in a polygamous marriage. In the peasant sector, the amount of a man's wealth often correlates directly with the number of wives he has. Polygamy gives a man a large reserve of unpaid labour and makes him the envy of other men. Thus, for a hunger-stricken and desperate family — usually it is the father who is anxious to

marry off a daughter as the means of survival — there is no shortage of would-be-polygamists. For a young girl, it is a high price to pay for the benefit of others, not herself. It must also be a cause of great sorrow and anguish for the mother as she watches helplessly.

Prostitution is increasing among women, particularly unmarried mothers, in an effort to earn income to support their family. Prostitution carries with it the ever-present danger of sexually-transmitted diseases, including HIV/AIDS. Other women face the danger of infection by promiscuous husbands and/or boyfriends.

Health impacts

Figure 3 illustrates a situation where progressive lowering of the water table due to drought leads to the reduction of gardening activities as wells and boreholes dry up. This has adverse consequences for the nutritional status of the family.

Another consequence is that access to clean water for domestic purposes will be difficult as water points get farther and farther away. Women will not have time to collect sufficient water to meet the family's needs. The consequent reduction in domestic and personal hygiene has obvious implications for health. Poor health, in turn, results in reduced agricultural productivity and consequent food shortages.

The increased mortality of domestic animals means that there will be less milk and meat for the family, with very serious effects on nutrition and health. The loss of draught power and resultant increase in the exhausting work of hand-tillage ultimately takes a toll on the women's health. It is likely that some women's life expectancy has been adversely affected by drought.

Food shortages also pose health risks to pregnant mothers and their unborn babies; and poor nutrition in the early years can have life-long consequences for young

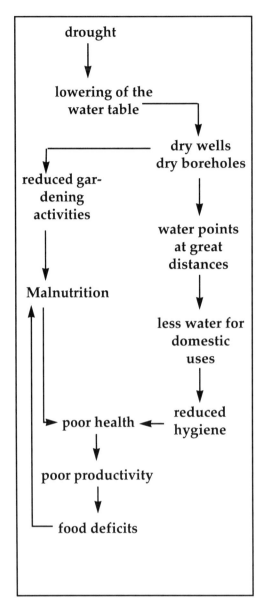

Figure 3: Health impacts of drought

they go to hospital to seek antenatal care, and many women do not go to the hospital at all, for this reason. The inevitable consequence will be increased levels of maternal mortality as the combination of under-nourishment and inadequate antenatal care takes its toll.

Drought-induced poverty also results in reduced access to medical care. Cost-recovery measures were introduced for health services as part of the Economic Reform Programme. Many women and their children cannot now afford medical care because their sources of income — crop surpluses — were wiped out by the drought.

Policy and planning implications

Drought relief and rehabilitation of food production must respond to the needs of women farmers in a manner that increases their capacity to withstand the effects of drought, at the same time reducing the burden of reproductive work. Future relief and rehabilitation programmes should aim at:

1 Meeting immediate food needs.
2 Strengthening women's role as farmers in their own right.
3 Introducing environmentally-sustainable long-term solutions to food deficits.

Current programmes are heavily biased towards short-term solutions such as food handouts, work projects and supplementary feeding schemes. Such interventions may immediately improve the material conditions of life in the existing drought situation, but do not empower women to fend for themselves in a future drought.

In future, reform programmes should be introduced alongside the traditional solutions to drought-related problems, with a view to improving the position of

girls. Girls who are healthy and well-fed during their own childhood and teenage years have fewer problems in pregnancy and at childbirth.

It should also be noted that rural hospitals do not provide food to mothers-in-waiting and their attendants. Because of food shortages at home, these mothers cannot take much food with them when women as farmers. Women should enjoy the same rights to arable land as men, the same access to extension services and agricultural credit, and equal control of agricultural produce and income. This will increase women's ability to plan for and maintain greater food self-sufficiency at household level, with cumulative effects at local level. While nothing can prevent drought, such reforms would enable women to plan for food production and make provision for a possible drought in the following season.

The effects of drought can be reduced through environmental-protection programmes, such as controlled-grazing schemes, reforestation projects, gully-reclamation projects, construction of silt traps, and construction of dams for irrigation purposes. Such programmes will reduce overgrazing and denudation of the land as well as improve the organic content and moisture-retention capacity of the soil, and should be in the form of on-going programmes rather than food-for-work projects in drought periods.

The combined effects of the socio-economic reforms and environmental protection programmes proposed here would improve women's socio-economic status and enhance their agricultural productivity. In turn, the role of women farmers in ensuring food self-sufficiency and food security would be strengthened, to the benefit of their families and society as a whole.

It would be wise to maintain a reasonable level of preparedness at national level to respond to severe drought. We now know that drought is a recurrent phenomenon. There is therefore no need to be caught unprepared. Both government and NGOs should allocate resources for appropriate contingency plans. Such plans would include a stand-by Drought Relief Fund or a Foodgrains Bank, or both. To facilitate effective food-distribution, a system of roads and convenient storage and distribution points should be established. This would avoid the costs of foreign loans to fund drought-relief operations in a country that is quite capable of feeding itself; or the embarrassing situation where existing food reserves cannot be delivered to starving people because of the poor road network.

Above all, contingency drought-relief plans should recognise the existing burden of reproductive work on women, rather than assume that women have an unlimited capacity to sustain this burden.

In short, what is being advocated is gender-sensitive forward planning for the prevention of food deficits in the event of drought. Where such food deficits are unavoidable, food distribution systems should be sensitive to women's existing burdens, and should not lose sight of the need to empower women to produce their own food as far as possible in future.

This paper was presented at a workshop on drought organised by the Zimbabwe Women's Resource Centre and Network in December 1992

Testimonies from Zaire

translated by Amby Hussein

Since autumn 1992 harassment of people of Kasaian origin in Shaba (formerly Katanga) in southern Zaire has resulted in massive displacement. More than 150,000 people have fled north into East and West Kasai, using whatever transport they could find. In October 1992 a Comite de Co-ordination des Refoules (CCR) was set up by local churches, non-governmental organisations (NGOs), and representatives of local authorities in Kananga. The CCR organises a transit facility where those arriving by train are registered and cared for, and are then either housed locally or channelled back to their areas of origin. Many of those arriving are in poor physical and psychological health; they are being fed with great difficulty and sacrifice by their extended families and local churches. Almost the only help they have received so far has come through the CCR. Oxfam has a sub-office in Kananga and has been assisting the CCR. Oxfam staff asked women to record their experience of being 'repatriated' from Shaba. Extracts from their accounts appear below.

Forced out of Shaba: Jeanne Walelu Bilolo

Since 1991 there has been an influx of young people from Katanga into the Likasi area. The Katanga press assured us that they were our fellow countrymen and said that we should welcome them. A few months after their arrival, the troubles exploded all around Likasi.

Kasaian refugees from the places where there had been disturbances told us how they were threatened, how they had lost all their possessions, and how people had been killed by machetes or burnt alive in their houses. These Kasaian refugees had walked long distances, carrying children on their backs and bundles on their heads.

After they had settled down in Likasi, there was a short period of calm and everyone hoped that the situation had stabilised. But one day we saw lines of people coming from the town of Likasi, who had much the same stories to tell. The young people from Katanga were burning houses, killing people, and destroying property.

The traders who had shops in town used them as refuges: during the day they were shops where goods were sold and at night they turned into shelters. Those who didn't know anyone they could find safety with, fled to the station. This was all happening in the rainy season; the worst time of year to be made homeless. Likasi finished up being divided into two parts, with most of the town and the settlements at the station for the Kasaians and the rest of the town being only for Katangans.

I am married and have nine children. We took in more than ten refugee families at our house, relatives and friends, and

*Displaced Kasaian families, on their long journey
to safety.*   SIMON TOWNSLEY/KATZ

none of these families had fewer than five
children. The house became a real stable, or
should I say a depot, since all the furniture
was piled up in corners; some people slept
in the bedrooms, some in the living room,
more in the garage; there were even people
sleeping in the kitchen. When the cooking
was being done it was like a lodging house
with everyone preparing food on their own
hearth.

During the day things in the house were
a bit better, as many people went about
their normal daily business. At night the
whole area was covered by a cloud of
smoke from the cooking fires, which made
it difficult to breathe.

To have a wash you had to get up at one
o'clock in the morning because there was
only one shower; the last person got a
shower at two in the afternoon. Many
people became ill with dysentery, measles,
and other diseases.

Our plot was shared with two other
families, one from Bakongo and the other
from Katanga (Basonga). Our neighbours
put up with the increase in our numbers

for the first month but eventually they
couldn't handle it any more because they
couldn't even have a wash comfortably
when they wanted one. All the places
where you could sit and relax were
occupied by refugees. In the end, we
decided we had to get out.

The authorities provided one free train a
week to take the refugees to their home
areas. The Kasaians were afraid and
suspicious of the first train, but a few
people took the train and went to Kasai. It
was only after the third train that we were
brave enough to leave Katanga, having
heard of the safe arrival of our friends who
had gone before.

At last it was our turn to leave Katanga.
We travelled in dreadful conditions. There
was no chance of being together in one
compartment, as we were a family of nine
children and two adults. There wasn't
enough food for the journey, and we
hadn't a penny to buy any. The children
had to stand up most of the way. It was
difficult to find any water to drink on
arriving in Katangan villages, and the
overcrowding and the heat made us faint. I
couldn't look after the children properly,
nor keep an eye on my possessions, A lot of
things were stolen, including clothes and
cooking utensils. The children were in a
really bad state, hungry and exhausted,
their feet swollen and sore with having to
stand up for so long.

During the journey there were many
deaths, particularly among the children
and the elderly who couldn't stand the
heat, the lack of air, and the overcrowding.
The train stopped more than five times in
order to bury the bodies of those who had
died. The journey took two weeks instead
of the two or three days it would have
taken in normal times.

When at last we arrived in Kananga we
celebrated because we were all safe back
home among our families, from whom we
had been away for years. We very quickly
got used to the new way of life, though it

was strange at first having to pass the night in the dark because there was no electricity or hurricane lanterns, and having to climb hills to get water from springs. We are still unemployed because we can't find jobs round here.

Kasaian women in Kolwezi: Felicite Tshikwakwa and Leontine Tumba

The root cause of the deterioration in the economic and social situation for women is the tribal hatred incited by various political groupings.

In March 1993 all Kasaian women were banned from working in the economic sector (markets, shops, sale of fish, vegetables) and later, were dismissed from their jobs in offices, cafes, schools, hospitals, and shops; and worst of all, were driven from their homes.

Young hooligans, high on drugs and alcohol, armed themselves with machetes, knives, spears, whips, sticks, and cans of petrol. Incited by Katangan leaders, the young assassins were dressed up in red headbands and painted with multicoloured paints, like traditional warriors.

Faced with this horde of young thugs shouting war cries in the streets and the factories, reclaiming the land of their forefathers with a dramatic call to 'Kill the Kasaians' and 'Kasaians go home', we Kasaian women and children were terrified; we hid in our houses, crammed together like rats. Some Kasaian children who got caught up in these scenes of mayhem fled for their lives, others fell down exhausted, some were beaten to death in cold blood.

The Kasaians were driven out by verbal and physical violence and arson. There were terrible atrocities: houses were set alight, and everything in them, both goods and people, were burned up.

So we women, without shelter — and this was the rainy season — burdened with children of all ages, in tears, hungry and frightened, were directed towards the stations and ordered to take the train and return to Kasai. What a scene of desolation, thousands of men and women, children and old people, milling about like ants, trying to make some sort of shelter with what they had could find: blankets, jute sacks, shawls, cardboard boxes ... What shelter for people who used to have decent homes with a bedroom for the parents, the girls, and the boys, and with a lavatory!

Apart from the space where our few possessions were piled up, a shawl or piece of cardboard separated the parents' corner from the children's area. Everyone slept on the floor, on mattresses of cardboard or jute sacks, or on the damp ground. After a while the older boys and girls got fed up and went off to look for a bed elsewhere. This meant they were exposed to the danger of debauchery and prostitution, but we could do nothing to stop them.

At first, some families were able to buy food with money from the sale of the possessions which they had managed to save when they were driven out. When this source of funds was exhausted, people went hungry.

Some Kasaian women left the relative safety of the camp to try and find food in the fields abandoned by their community. The unlucky ones who strayed into the area controlled by the Katangan militia were beaten, raped, or killed. These atrocities put an end to going into the fields, and food became very scarce. All there was to eat was maize grains and bits of grilled manioc. The lack of protein made people start 'operation eat dog', so that by June 1993 it was rare to meet a dog at Kolwezi.

With the hunger, overcrowding and lack of hygiene in the camp, disease spread rapidly. The children and older people became weak and ill from kwashiorkor, vitamin deficiency, anaemia, and water-borne diseases such as dysentery, and many died. Some days, we buried up to 35 people. We buried our dead without shroud or coffin, sometimes in shallow communal graves. We were beginning to despair when one day the Red Cross arrived to care for the sick and to distribute food. More than 640 deaths were notified by the Red Cross between 20 March and 25 May 1993.

The Kasaians were denied access to dispensaries and health centres. All the Kasaian doctors and nurses had already been driven out. What shame for mothers who had to give birth in such conditions, with no privacy, in front of their own children! Health conditions improved after the Red Cross and Medecins sans Frontieres arrived at Kolwezi. They cared for the sick, Kasaianand Katangan alike.

Tribal hatred has reached the point where even the Katangan children hate the Kasaian children from the bottom of their hearts. People in mixed marriages faced terrible problems. The majority of Kasaian women married to Katangan men were driven out with their children. What could they do with so many children and without the support of the head of the family, in a patrilineal tradition? Some Kasaian women had never even been to Kasai. In the case of Kasaian men married to Katangan women, over 50 per cent of women agreed to go to Kasai with their husband; others preferred divorce.

Having escaped from the hell of Katanga by air, road or train, the refugee families heaved sighs of relief! But there were still a multiplicity of problems.

Most families came by train. Many families found themselves in reception centres where the conditions were the same as those in Kolwezi. Families without contacts in Kananga were taken by road to various rural areas in West Kasai, where the problems were even worse. Why doesn't someone give each family a tent, or an amount of money to help them build a house quickly, with the help of the villagers?

For those of us who decided to live in Kananga, there has been no help from the NGOs or the government to help us settle in. When we left Shaba we had to abandon houses which we had not managed to sell. Now, in Kananga the rents have tripled, and are unaffordable.

There were problems with obtaining water and food, but some sort of solution has been found. Clean drinking water is delivered in tanks. Given the number of people living in the reception centres, the women with young children have to queue up for water so long that they have little time left in the day to do anything else.

As for food, the ration of two meals a day which women used to get to feed their children, has been reduced to one meal a day. Families who have found a place to stay are not even entitled to this ration. The authorities seem to have forgotten that this town has been ransacked twice, and people have suffered badly. Our arrival made life even more difficult for people who had few resources left. The last distribution of flour to refugees gave a family of 12 to 14 children about 7 to 8 kilos of flour, or three days' supply at one meal per day. For a month now, the women have been asking themselves how they and their families are going to survive.

For many of us, with husbands out of work, there has been no income for months. Organisations working on humanitarian aid for refugees must take this problem seriously. Unless employment is created here the future is bleak. Will we have escaped sudden death, only to face a lingering death from poverty?

Emergency food distribution in Turkana

A developmental approach

Isobel Birch

This case study describes a method of food distribution currently in operation in Turkana district in north-west Kenya, which explores the potential of adopting a developmental approach to relief work. One important element is the attempt to take full account of the needs and position of women within Turkana society, and to reflect these within the programme's methodology.

Turkana is a semi-arid area with low and variable rainfall. A recent aerial survey estimates there to be 226,000 pastoralists in the district, the bedrock of whose economy is their livestock — cattle, goats, sheep and camels. This is supplemented by other forms of production such as seasonal sorghum growing and fishing, and by barter trade within and outside the district. In addition to the pastoral population there is an increasing proportion of sedentary or semi-sedentary Turkana for whom livestock management is of diminishing importance.

By the middle of 1992 Turkana was facing critical food shortages due partly to several years of drought and partly to restrictions in access to grazing, caused by insecurity along the border areas. A nutrition survey carried out by UNICEF in August 1992 revealed a district-wide malnutrition rate (less than 80 per cent weight for height) of 35 per cent. Supplementary feeding by UNICEF began in September and distributions of general rations by Oxfam and World Vision in November 1992.

A responsive programme

The programme design was based upon that developed by Oxfam in Uganda in the late 1980s and early 1990s and was implemented by Oxfam in Kenya in Samburu earlier in 1992. One of its key principles was that as far as possible the relief programme should incorporate a developmental approach — that it should seek to inform and involve beneficiaries, to respect and protect the lifestyle of pastoralists, and to take account of women's key role in food management within Turkana society.

A married or widowed woman in Turkana is responsible for the food needs of all her dependents attached to her *ekol* or day house. The *awi* is the livestock management unit which may be subdivided into several *ekols*. The male head of the household controls the *awi*, whereas the women or co-wives control the food supply for their individual *ekols*. Each woman has responsibility for the milk supply from the animals and also plays a role in their management, particularly in health care and watering. Her responsibility for food security covers both animal products and food acquired from other sources.

The food distribution programme attempted to reinforce rather than undermine this system of social organisation. During the initial registration process women were registered first. Each

Herding livestock, beside a homestead in Turkana. Women play an important role in the pastoral economy, being involved in milk production, and health care and watering of animals. IAN LEGGETT/OXFAM

member of a woman's *ekol* was registered with her, and each person named in the register was entitled to receive the same ration. The food is distributed directly to each individual woman on behalf of all her dependents, thus ensuring that it reaches the person most directly concerned with the household's food supply. Informal interviews with women indicate that they prefer this more equitable approach to one in which the same food ration is distributed to households regardless of their size.

The method of distribution is a transparent and simple one, which tries to avoid potential diversion or unfairness in the provision of food. Distributions are carried out in an open place and attended in the main by the registered women (those receiving the food) and by male elders. Rations are publicly announced before the distribution and the names of those registered are also called out in turn. A

system of scooping is used which is easily followed and supervised. A jerry can is cut to the appropriate weight for the monthly ration so that one scoop of food equals one person's entitlement. Thus a woman with five children knows that she is eligible to receive six scoops — one for her plus five for her children.

The relief committee

An important feature of the programme is the presence of an elected relief committee of elders at each of the distribution points. The committee acts as the consignee of food for that centre and has responsibility for the conduct of the monthly distribution, including supervision of the scooping. Oxfam encouraged the election of women onto these committees, and on the whole, most of them have a fairly balanced membership of men and women. The presence of a woman on a committee is no guarantee that women's needs will be taken into account, but during Oxfam's meetings with the committees the women members are encouraged to participate fully and to express their opinions. Most of the women on the committees demonstrate an impressive level of responsibility and commitment to their role.

Committee elections and community meetings tend to take place once people have gathered before the monthly distribution begins. Although the male/female dynamic within the community may still tend to prioritise men's views over women's, the fact that more women than men attend the distribution (since they are the ones registered as beneficiaries) *de facto* means that at committee elections it is mainly the women who are voting for their representatives.

The active involvement and participation of women was thus a central objective in attempting to fulfil the aim of incorporating a developmental approach in the relief programme. Another developmental principle was that the lifestyle of pastoralists should be respected and protected as far as possible. The programme is decentralised, with 63 different dropping-points across the four northern divisions of the district. This means that the food is taken as close as possible to the beneficiaries, thus minimising disruption to normal patterns of life and reducing the distances people have to walk to distributions. There are currently 149,509 people registered in the centres, the furthest of which is 233 miles from the main district office in Lodwar. At each centre an Oxfam monitor or assistant monitor — both men and women — acts as Oxfam's main link with that community, and monitors the programme in that centre.

There are also several strategies to accommodate the mobility of pastoralists. There is a facility to move names from

Food distribution, Turkana. Women receive food on behalf of all their dependents.   GEOFF SAYER/OXFAM

register to register, and with the more mobile groups the monitor negotiates a mutually-convenient point where the food can be delivered each month. When water and pasture become scarce some groups will split their herds and separate. In such situations the food for that centre is also divided and appropriate proportions despatched to the new grazing areas. The objective is to avoid undermining the traditional survival strategies and grazing patterns of the Turkana, which include the splitting of herds at times of stress.

Strengthening the pastoral economy

In addition to relieving hunger and suffering, an important programme objective was to strengthen and support the pastoral economy. It was reasoned that if alternative sources of food were made widely available throughout the pastoral sector, people might be able to avoid further selling or slaughtering of animals for food. This was one of the justifications for the extensive and largely untargeted registration of the population: all but wage-earners were registered. Data from the district drought monitoring unit (the Turkana Drought Contingency Planning Unit) supports this argument and indicates that herd growth is slow but positive, the price of livestock and livestock products has risen, and the rates of sale and slaughter have fallen. The intention is that food distributions at some level will continue until the underlying food situation improves and recovery is seen to be taking place. The aim is to demonstrate an approach to the use of food aid which looks beyond nutritional indicators and acknowledges the wider socio-economic impact of that food on a community.

There are clearly limitations to the extent of community involvement in a large-scale food distribution programme — partly because the logistical arrangements

tend to be centralised and partly because of the involvement of other organisations which may not share the same approach. The relief committees in Turkana have minimal control over the food supply, which is determined by a succession of donors and agencies long before it even reaches the district capital. However, one of the issues which Oxfam is keen to explore in future is the potential of the committees to take part in both short-to-medium term representational and lobbying activities — for example, around food allocations — and in longer-term development work. One of the most rewarding aspects of the programme has been the way in which committee members have come to understand their role and to use this to challenge those in authority if they feel their position to be under threat.

The kind of principles espoused in development work do not necessarily have to be sacrificed in emergency situations.

The programme in Turkana, like that in Samburu and those in northern Uganda before it, is trying to show that the kind of principles espoused in development work do not necessarily have to be sacrificed in emergency situations. In certain circumstances it is possible to carry out relief work in ways which inform and involve beneficiaries, which reinforce and respect their lifestyle, and which above all reflect an awareness of the differing needs and roles of men and women within society.

Isobel Birch is Programme Manager for Oxfam's Turkana Relief Programme in north-west Kenya.

Forty seconds that shook their world
The 1993 earthquake in India

Editor's note: There was a massive and generous response within India to the earthquake disaster in Maharashtra, and many volunteers came to the affected areas to offer assistance. The majority of volunteers were men, and it was important to ensure that this did not mean, as so often has been the case, that the experience and particular needs of women were not fully identified and addressed. In the first weeks after the disaster women suffered increased stress because of the lack of privacy. There was no opportunity to communicate in privacy with partners, families and intimate friends. Other problems related to women's domestic roles as managers of food and water. There were complaints about the poor quality of the relief grain, the lack of fresh vegetables, and the difficulties and cost of cooking with kerosene rather than on the wood-fired stoves, destroyed in the disaster. The use of buckets rather than water-pots made the water more liable to contamination, and the delivery of water by tanker was not well-organised, leading to a free-for-all, and spillage. The following reports describe some of the problems women faced. Eileen Maybin notes the especial vulnerability of widows, and the denial of their rights to land and property. Manisha Tokle considers some of the practical difficulties, and women's anxieties for the future.

1 Rebuilding shattered lives

Eileen Maybin

The earthquake which rocked the southern Indian state of Maharashtra on September 30 spared no section of the community: rich and poor, Muslim and Hindu, artisan and farm labourer, are still grieving over their dead and injured.

Yet even in the event of such an indiscriminate tragedy, it is clear that women and children have suffered more than the menfolk — not only because they died in greater numbers (since traditionally men will often sleep outdoors) but because many of them have been left in an extremely vulnerable position in the aftermath of the earthquake.

Chandrakala Dagadu was fast asleep in the small village of Matola when the mud and stone walls of her house came tumbling down around her, destroyed by vibrations from the earthquake, which measured 6.4 on the Richter scale. Chandrakala, pinned down by the weight of the debris, would have suffocated like 20,000 other people if she had not been pulled from the wreckage of her home by survivors of the disaster, which left 100,000 homeless.

Before the earthquake Chandrakala lived with her husband's family, who owned several acres where they grew *jowar* (a local grain), sunflowers and sugar cane. Like most of the small-scale farmers in the area, they made a reasonably good living by selling their crops. The black cotton soil provides rich agricultural land around the 82 villages in the two districts affected by the earthquake, Latur and Osmanabad. With their earnings, Chandrakala could afford to send her children to school. She would spend her days with her sister-in-law and mother-in-law, going about the household chores or working in the fields.

But Chandrakala's entire world collapsed on September 30. She lost her husband, her two sons, her parents-in-law, her sister-in-law, and her nephew. She now stares blankly into the distance, barely responding to questions and seldom eating.

'Chandrakala might be able to cope with her grief better if she could go back to her own family for emotional support and sympathy but custom dictates that she stay with her husband's family, so she has to remain with the only other surviving family member, her brother-in-law,' says Leo Bashyam, Christian Aid's Project Officer for South India. A partner organisation, Action for Agricultural Renewal in Maharashtra (AFARM), started sending teams of volunteers into the area to console and counsel victims immediately after the disaster happened. The teams are currently looking at each individual's circumstances to try to offer suitable comfort.

'As well as counselling, hundreds of widows and children need legal advice and help to understand their claims on property and compensation for lost family members,' says Dr Ghare, chairperson of AFARM. 'Otherwise they may fall victim to greedy relatives turned fortune-hunters.'

Although the government froze title-deeds to property a few days after the earthquake, there are fears that widows

Devastation in Killari, a small town in the area affected by the earthquake. PAUL SHERLOCK/OXFAM

and orphans could still be tricked out of property. 'It could be quite a lucrative move for a male relative to take in a widow or orphan who should inherit property and has lost several family members,' Dr Ghare explains. For each person dead, the government has promised to pay 50,000 rupees (over £1,000) — a sizeable sum in rural India.

'It is important that appropriate aid is sent ... and that it is distributed fairly and sensitively,

The plight of the victims of the earthquake touched the hearts of vast numbers of people throughout India and abroad. For the first time, technology was able to flash the pictures of a major Indian earthquake onto people's televisions. In India civil servants in many government ministries donated a day's salary, national newspapers raised huge amounts of money with their appeals, and people from a wide range of groups, from the All India Bank Employees' Association to the Rig Owners' Association of Solapur, rushed to the affected area with lorries full of food and clothing.

The spontaneous outpouring of concern from India and the international community was impressive but unfortunately sometimes inappropriate — the second-hand designer jeans and *salwar kamesz* sent from New Delhi will not be worn by the traditional people of Latur and Osmanabad, who also balk at unfamiliar plastic buckets, woollen blankets, and high-vitamin biscuits sent from Europe.

'It is important that appropriate aid is sent after an emergency like this and that it is distributed fairly and sensitively,' says Dr Ghare. 'Otherwise, people's trauma can be compounded.' Much of the aid which flooded into the area from organisations unaccustomed to relief situations was

handed out in a haphazard way — some people received duplicate sets of cooking pots and bedding while many women and children, unable or too reserved to make their way to the queues, were left with practically nothing.

'The needs are so great', says Dr Ghare, 'that it is important for experienced development agencies to ensure the most vulnerable receive the support necessary.'

Ashish Gram Rachna Trust, the Institute of Health Management, is concentrating on women and children. It works with women like the elderly Kasi who, without extra family help, could not manage to harvest the family crops which were ripe on the family land two weeks after the earthquake.

The Institute is planning to train these women in health care and water management. Teams of women will monitor the areas around new wells to ensure these community facilities are kept in good order. Women will also monitor the maintenance of hand-pumps to ensure that any small repairs are carried out when necessary and before major damage is caused.

The Institute is also providing books, slates, school bags, uniforms, raincoats and scholarships to help children restart classes in makeshift schools.

Asked what her most pressing needs were just 48 hours after the disaster, which left her in hospital along with her 15-day-old baby, Chayabai Kamble, from the village of Killhari, said she wanted her two older children to be able to go back to school.

'I have lost my home, I have lost everything, I feel as if I have no future,' said Chayabai. 'But I know it is important for my children to begin their education again — otherwise, we will be feeling the effects of the earthquake for a long time to come.'

Eileen Maybin is Asia/Pacific Group Journalist for Christian Aid.

A woman cleaning cooking utensils, salvaged from the ruins of her house.   JOE HUMAN/OXFAM

2 Some problems women are facing

Manisha Tokle

Fear

The women are very afraid. There is a constant feeling of insecurity and uncertainty about the earthquake. They can not concentrate on any work. The dreams they had about the future have been shattered. There is fear in their minds: if we try to rebuild, and if it takes place again ... what then? The sowing was delayed by one month, so they also fear crop failure. They are confused about everything they are doing and are not sure whether it is right.

Health problems

Most of the women have health problems of one kind or the other, especially the ones who have undergone tubectomy, who suffer pain. This could be because of their tensions and psychological problems. Problems with menstrual periods and bleeding due to tensions and shocks are very common. The absence of nurses and gynaecologists adds to the anxiety of the women, and the problems are aggravated.

Sanitation (bathrooms and latrines)

Most of the camps do not have bathrooms and latrines. The women are very uncomfortable when they cannot bathe for days. They can only have a 'full bath' (when they can wash their hair) every 15 days or so. It becomes even more of a problem at the time of the menstrual cycle. Whenever they take a bath they have to do it in a limited space in front or behind their shelter before day-break.

Scarcity of water

Water is supplied to many villages by tankers, but in some villages there is no provision of water. The women suffer most because of this; they have to stand in queues to get water. If there is a tank in the camp it is small and by the time women from the other end of the camp reaches the tank it is empty. Children do not bathe in the house, due to lack of water, but in puddles around the village.

Destitute women and widows

This group is severely affected. In many cases the help received by these women is swallowed up by neighbours or relatives. An attempt was made to evacuate such women from their shelters, in one of the villages. These women do not have any emotional or economic support.

Uncertainty about the future of the children

Women feel that in the present conditions they have no food and no money, and they are very sceptical about the future of their children. They can do nothing but see their children standing in queues collecting help coming from outside, and worry about their schooling. Many women are afraid that if the children stay here they will turn into beggars; and if they stay in the village, they will be struck by an earthquake and suffer the same fate as their parents. Many women are sending their children to the cities in the hope that they will go to school there and have a better future.

Unemployment

Women labourers do not have employment in the village. Skilled workers also face the problem of unemployment; for example, a woman tailor's clients have ready-made clothes (thanks to relief supplies), or her machine is out of order or destroyed. They want somebody to get orders for them from outside, which they will fulfil. They feel that employment should be available

Priyanka ('precious one'); she survived for five days buried under debris.   Joe Human/Oxfam

locally. They could also do craft work on clothes and knitting. Adding to their problems is the fact that the temporary shelters have not been provided with doors, so they cannot leave their houses to seek employment outside.

Beliefs about the earthquake

'This earthquake is the starting point of the destruction ahead. Now another earthquake will tear the earth. All these villages will be buried. All those who are dead have become ghosts and they will not let us live in peace. This is the result of our sins committed in previous times or due to crimes committed in earlier life.' This is what people are thinking now. This type of belief is more common in women. Uncertainty, instability and illiteracy are the roots of these fears. Lack of scientific information about the earthquake are nourishing these beliefs.

In the villages affected by the earthquake, it is the women who are most affected by the lack of water, food, electricity, shelter. They are the ones who are the victims in reality.

Manisha Tokle is a woman worker with the Rural Development Centre.

A disaster-preparedness workshop in Pakistan

From a report prepared by Yasmin Ahmed

In May 1993 Oxfam Pakistan and PATTAN, an NGO set up to undertake flood-preparedness and mitigation, relief and development work in the riverine areas of Punjab, held a disaster-preparedness workshop. In September 1992, floods had devastated much of Pakistan, and the purpose of the workshop was to help NGO workers to prepare for any future emergency by collective reflection on the lessons learnt in the floods, and practical training in disaster response techniques and planning for future disaster. Gender issues were an important focus in the workshop and participants unanimously agreed that in future they would undertake all relief goods distributions through women and give high priority to incorporating women in the relief teams. As preparation for this, they resolved to enhance the participation of women in their development team. The slogan was: 'No women, no team'!

Food aid

A participant said that a survey carried out after food distribution in 1992 revealed that a lot of women, such as widows, second wives, and women whose husbands were away from home, did not get relief. The solution was to consider the women to be more suitable representatives of the family and distribute relief goods through them.

In response to the point that in certain areas women are bound by custom and tradition and cannot come out to receive emergency relief even in a disaster, the participants from PATTAN said that if women are included in the survey teams of relief organisations, women will talk to the team about the problems they face; and will come to get relief goods if women are included in the distribution team. There was a vital need for change in the attitude of men working in NGOs. It is essential for them to realise the importance of including women members in their team and working through them in an emergency.

Gender issues

The purpose of the session was to explore and analyse the implications of gender in an emergency situation.

First, the participants were divided into groups and asked to imagine a day in the life of a husband and wife in a low-income family and chart the tasks performed by each in one day. Common aspects to emerge were that in the rural community women work longer hours and do a greater number of chores. Most of the work in the reproductive role is done by women, whereas most of men's work is done outside the home. Men have more leisure time; women sleep from two to four hours less than men do.

Then, in a role play, participants explored what it felt like to be ignored and excluded from decision making — the common experience of women.

A third exercise focused specifically on the problems faced by women during the 1992 flood. Participants were divided into three groups.

Group 1: A men's group was asked to identify women's problems during the flood and suggest solutions. The group identified three categories of problems, economic, social, and domestic. They suggested practical solutions, including loans, the creation of shelter to provide for purdah, and better-targeted relief, given directly to women. They also stressed the need for women's involvement in NGOs to tackle women's problems. Domestic problems were listed as practical difficulties of lack of food, water and clothing.

Group 2: A men's group was asked to identify problems faced by men during a disaster. This group also saw economic problems as significant, although they too highlighted anxieties about family needs. Solutions were the provision of employment, and for men to discuss their problems together and try to make contact with relief agencies at different levels.

Group 3: A women's group was asked to identify the problems faced by women and suggest solutions. They came up with a long list of varied problems, almost all related to the needs and nurture of the family. They included physical needs such as food and water, but also concerns about children and the elderly, and the protection of young daughters. Health problems included diseases resulting from unhygienic conditions, the needs of women who were pregnant or breastfeeding, and care in childbirth. Economic problems noted were the loss of savings and dowries for daughters, and worry about debt payments. They also mentioned the lack of

purdah; problems about reconstruction of houses, and anxieties about the future. The solutions they suggested were to include women in relief teams, who would understand women's specific problems, to distribute relief through women, and to form women's committees to look at women's problems more widely.

In the discussion that followed the participants concluded that the problems of women are different from the problems of men in an emergency situation, and that no emergency relief or development programme can be successful without the involvement of women. Women's participation in socio-economic development depends upon the attitude of men, and it is important for men to change their attitude towards women. Women should be respected as individuals equal to men.

Recommendations

The recommendations presented by participants in this session were:
• Women should be included in NGOs as members who can look into development and emergency relief projects from the perspective of gender.
• Men should respect women's unpaid labour and share household responsibilities because women carry a double and in some cases a triple burden.
• In an emergency relief good should be distributed through women.
• If we really wish to bring about a positive change in the status and condition of women then an emergency situation can be used to break the conventions and tradition which prevent women from participating in the process of social development.

(Taken from: Proceedings of the Oxfam Pakistan/PATTAN Disaster Workshop, 23-27 May 1993, Bhurban, Murree, prepared for Oxfam by Yasmin Ahmed.)

Sudanese refugees in Koboko

Environmental health interventions

Joy Morgan

During August 1993, 50,000 Sudanese fled south over the border into Uganda. Some fled from fear of air-attack by government forces, others had been displaced many times, and their homes raided and burned. Women had been raped, their children killed, and cattle stolen in inter-factional fighting Many had left behind them all of their possessions, and crops ripening in their fields. Most of them were Kakwa people and many of them were Christians. The Sudanese found themselves in Idi Amin's home town, which until two years ago had been evacuated because of fighting between Ugandan factions. The Ugandans in the area had only recently returned from their refuges in Zaire and southern Sudan and knew what it was like to be a refugee.

Some agencies which had been working in southern Sudan were also displaced along with the refugees. They continued to provide health care and education services, but there was an urgent need for improvements to water supplies and for hygiene promotion. The provision of water for the large population settling on forested hills bisected by rivers, was complicated to plan and implement. The Oxfam Uganda Emergency team offered to help. They requested additional technical advice to assist with the first phase of the emergency intervention. This was my chance to find out whether the advice I had been giving to field personnel on environmental health, including the integration of gender sensitivity into technical programmes, was appropriate in emergencies.

Assessing the needs

It was difficult to obtain reliable statistics on the refugee population, and a counting exercise was carried out by UNHCR and the Ugandan Red Cross Society in which Oxfam assisted. The results from a small sample of households suggested that about half the displaced population was under the age of 15; there were more adult males than females — unusual for a refugee camp, where there are often less than 20 per cent of adult males — and, also unusual in a refugee situation, more households headed by men than by women.

The count was initiated, not only because there had been no clear idea of numbers of people and locations, but also as a way of dividing the refugees up into small groups with elected leaders, to improve the distribution system and make it more equitable. When I first arrived in the camp I witnessed the distribution of soap. A small riot was occurring because UNHCR had brought only one lorry load of soap and the refugees thought that was not enough. As we passed, a woman attracted our attention. She was Angelina

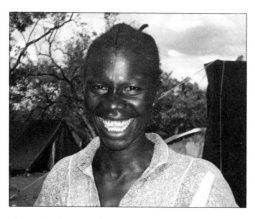

Mary Anite, a Sudanese trained as a spring technician.   JOY MORGAN/OXFAM

Dusuman, a Church elder who had been translating for Judy Adoko, the Oxfam Gender Officer, when Judy had visited the camp several weeks before. Angelina explained what was happening: items were distributed in a haphazard way to self-elected leaders, who were then to distribute to several thousand refugees. There was corruption and a certain amount of pocket-lining going on. Angelina asked me what I was doing there, and I explained that I had been asked to help in improving the drinking water situation. Angelina told me that she knew Mary Anite, a Sudanese woman trained by Oxfam Sudan in 1985 as a spring technician, and promised to introduce her to me.

Water supply for the camp: first steps

Before my arrival, the Oxfam team had already started to look at water sources. There were some small springs but they looked too small for the numbers of people to be supplied. It had been decided to pump water from the Kochi River to a high point in the camp, treat it and distribute it by gravity in pipes to tapstands. Refugee women had told Judy that they were familiar with drinking chlorinated water, so no problem was anticipated. The engineering operation took several weeks and water was beginning to flow soon after I arrived. To our disappointment, women would walk past the tapstands to collect water from tiny springs by the market place, which were obviously contaminated, because they preferred the taste of unchlorinated spring water.

Spring protection

When I met Mary Anite, we looked for springs which would be worth protecting and were likely to stay flowing throughout the dry season. Mary introduced me to Abrahiem Khamis, her former supervisor, and together they started to identify potential springs and discuss them with the local population. The Ugandan women were not able to tell us which of the springs were permanent through the driest seasons as they themselves had only recently returned from the Sudan. But they were keen to identify good, permanent springs which could be protected by the refugees and used to supply their houses as well as the camps. We located several springs outside the camp on high land, and a swamp was chosen as the most promising source.

When work started on the spring, Mary would work alongside the male and female labourers to make sure that as the swamp was cleared, the source of the spring was not damaged. Some of these labourers, including six women, were to be trained as spring technicians themselves. Within a week, clean spring water was flowing and the swamp was beginning to dry up. Refugee women would walk up from the camp to collect their water from this new and improved source.

Community participation in planning the supply

I wanted to use participatory mapping in order to work out exactly where to locate

Women collecting water from a spring on the outskirts of the camp. Construction work is going on to protect the spring.   Joy Morgan/Oxfam

the tapstands. Simon Ameny, the Oxfam Emergency Programme Officer asked the community to draw the locations of their houses, plots and landmarks, on the ground. Women and men enjoyed mapping their new home environment and then deciding where would be the best place for taps; one tapstand with six taps would serve a population of about 1000 people. The women wanted the tapstands centrally located so that nobody had too far to walk, and they took us to show us the places that they had decided on. The refugees wanted to help in digging the trench, fixing the pipes and assembling the tapstands. It was now up to Saidi Kikoya, Oxfam Emergency Technician, to survey the pipelines and get the water where people wanted it. That was not always easy, and one tapstand had to be moved down the hill slightly to make the water flow faster.

Within another two weeks, water was flowing out of the spring into a collection chamber, where a tap was installed for use by local people. Any excess water flowed down a pipe, to be stored in a reservoir tank ready to supply demand at the tapstands. We couldn't understand why women were walking past the taps, past the tank, up to the spring to collect their water. When asked, they said that the water tasted of chili pepper, that we had put aspirin in the water, or that a rat had fallen into the tank! Where had we gone wrong? It was time to call in Angelina again.

The importance of health promotion

Angelina had not realised that the taps were working already. She spent the next morning going round the area talking to people she met and telling them that the water was safe to drink — nothing added and nothing taken away. Gregory, the government health educator did the same.

'Within a few days, demand for the spring water from the taps was high and everyone seemed happy with the system.'   JOY MORGAN/OXFAM

He gave a short talk to the residents and also spoke at a meeting of refugee group leaders about the merits of spring water. Within a few days demand for the spring water from the taps was high and everyone seemed happy with the system. Who knows if it was the passage of time, the health education messages, the encouragement of Angelina, their respected women representative, or some other cultural factor, that worked the change?

Community responsibility

The Ugandan Red Cross Society had some 65 Ugandan volunteers working in the camp. Some were undertaking a health education role. We had talked with them about the possibility of them putting on some street theatre emphasising the need for the tapstand users to look after the tapstands, in particular to stop wastage of water and maintain the tapstand areas in a clean and well drained condition. After several weeks, the drama was performed. The Red Cross Volunteers played their

parts as naughty children playing with the taps and leaving them running, they played the parts of mosquitoes and flies thriving in the waste water swamp and being a nuisance to the tapstand users, one actor was so irritated by the mosquitoes that she lost her footing on the muddy tapstand and fell over breaking her water container. The large crowd of men, women and children enjoyed the performance. It was rounded off by a Red Cross health educator appearing and asking the audience whether situations like this could happen, and if so, what they thought needed to be done. The audience were quick to say that it was happening in the camp already and that they needed to select a tapstand committee of six men and six women for each tapstand. They were elected there and then. These committee members will be the key contact persons for further hygiene promotion activities in future.

The committees were quick to say that they wanted to understand the system fully and to be able to make simple repairs themselves. They have since been walked all along the system and shown how the technology works. I have every confidence that these committees will provide the enthusiasm to keep the systems functioning effectively for a long time to come.

In low-conflict emergency situations like this one, I am convinced that women can fully participate in the decision-making processes of environmental health interventions. Activities like the selection of water sources, the location of water points and maintenance of the system can give some control in a situation where dependency on outside help predominates. The key is to talk with and listen to women's opinions and to observe their behaviour carefully.

Joy Morgan is the Emergency Support Engineer in the Specialist Support Team of Oxfam's Emergencies Department.

Women refugees in Bangladesh

Gawher Nayeem Wahra

In 1991-2 about 300,000 Rohingya refugees from Mayanmar (Burma) took shelter in south-east Bangladesh. Muslims from the Rakhaine state, numbering between one and two million, are distinct linguistically from the Buddhist Burman majority of Myanmar. The repression of Muslims is part of a consistent pattern of human rights violations against all political opposition and dissent, and against vulnerable and weak sectors of the country's population, such as ethnic minorities, who the military authorities suspect may not support its nationalist ideology. Muslims from the Rakhaine state fled in similar numbers to Bangladesh in 1978 and were later repatriated after an agreement between the two countries was reached.

At first the government of Bangladesh showed remarkable hospitality and provided land and shelter to this large-scale influx. UNHCR was requested to assist in mid-February 1992. Oxfam's involvement was at first to fund health services, then at the urging of UNHCR, Oxfam brought in water equipment and engineers in April 1992 to provide water for some of the camps. Later Oxfam took on another wide-ranging project in the sector of sanitation and environmental health services in two of the camps where it had helped instal water supplies. This is rounded out with a health education programme.

Repatriation agreement

An agreement signed by the Governments of Bangladesh and Myanmar in late April of 1992 to repatriate all refugees over six months provided no provision for UNHCR supervision or involvement in the repatriation process on either side of the border. After several attempts by the UN at different levels the government of Bangladesh allowed UNHCR's protection officers to verify the 'voluntary' repatriation through individual interviews and access to repatriation transit camps in Bangladesh. Refugees wish to remain in Bangladesh until they are sure of their future safety in Myanmar and UNHCR's active involvement on the other side of the border. The government of Bangladesh is encouraging refugees' departure by ordering all NGOs to terminate employment of refugees, restricting movement between camps, and closing down the small makeshift shops inside and around the camps. Refugees are increasingly being confined to their camps and actively discouraged from using local markets.

Myanmar signed a Memorandum with UNHCR in November 1993 allowing them to monitor repatriation in Rohingya areas in Myanmar. UNHCR is now working out the detailed tasks and activities to implement the memorandum. Both UNHCR and Government of Bangladesh

The camp for Rohingya refugees in south–east Bangladesh.   HOWARD DAVIES/OXFAM

are expecting January 1994 to see the start of the accelerated repatriation.

Forced to 'volunteer': Amina's story

'When they started pushing they pushed us first, now you start pushing and again we are the first,' said Amina, a widow in her early forties with five children under 12, when armed police 'helped' her pack her belongings hurriedly on the way to a transit camp for 'voluntary repatriation' in September, 1992.

After the repatriation agreement between the two governments, the authorities instructed each 'camp-in-charge' to arrange for volunteers for repatriation. Each camp-in-charge had to fulfil a fixed quota by producing a weekly list of the refugees who were 'willing' to go back. The camp-in-charge have used a 'carrot and stick' policy to fulfil their quota. Most of the time they

are so desperate that they start with less carrot and more stick and end up with no carrot and all stick. Widows with children are the easiest victims of this voluntary repatriation operation.

I met Amina first in January 1992 in Dhechuapalnog area among the first group of refugees. At that time only the workers of Gonoshastya Kendra, an NGO with a long history of medical work dating back to the Liberation War, was working with the refugees. Its workers had started a survey and needs assessment. I asked a worker to help me as an interpreter as I wanted to talk with some women who came without husbands, father or a male guardian.

Amina had had to cross the border with her children as the members of the Burmese paramilitary force 'Lone Htein' started raiding their villages to collect the able-bodied people as forced labour. 'Lone Htein' were not happy with only able-bodied men, they took the women as well in their camps for 'household' work. They targeted women-headed families as the easiest sources when they were looking for young girls to take advantage of. First they asked for money in lieu of male labour, then livestock, then poultry. If nothing was available, they would take a girl. This happened to Amina. At first they took her life-savings of 500 kyats, two goats, and gold earrings. The second time, when she had nothing to offer, they asked her to hand over her 12-year-old daughter just for two or three days. 'I refused and cried. Then they took me to their camp and they kept me there the whole night. Next day they released me but took me again the following day for another two nights.'

Amina took a decision and crossed the River Naf for a secure life in Bangladesh and to protect her children from the hands of 'Lone Htein'. Crossing the border was traumatic. 'Lone Htein' confiscated her money (which she had borrowed from the village head man to meet the costs of the journey), her national registration cards, and her few possessions.

After eight months of refugee life in Bangladesh, moving from one shelter to another, Amina found herself again trapped by authorities against whom she was powerless. This time her 9-year-old son was caught red-handed by the Camp Guards breaking the law when he was trying to sell some pulses (which the refugees are given but don't like as food) to buy some vegetables and dried fish. (At that time dried fish was not in the food basket of UNHCR.) They confiscated the pulses and took him into custody. Hearing of the incident, Amina with their Mahjhi (head man), rushed to the camp office to plead for her son. The guards asked her to choose one of two options — either face the police case as her son broke the law, in which case the authorities would send him to jail; or list her name in the voluntary repatriation list and get herself ready for repatriation within a

week. 'Go back or face the trial': the solution was as simple as that. What could Amina do in such a situation? She was not ready to leave her only son in the hands of foreign police so she opted for repatriation. There are so many such Aminas still struggling in the camps.

The vulnerability of women refugees

Many of the women arrived with a history of rape, and came from divided families with lost husbands or children. They may have been unaccompanied, possibly pregnant or with VD, but they had little hope of being treated sympathetically by male doctors. They have found themselves in camps where the space for them to lead anything but the most restricted lives is unavailable, and where the level of curiosity at what they had been through made them the object of unwelcome attention from the media and local population.

It became very hard to find a safe place for women who suffered at the hands of the forces on the other side of the border; the same vulnerability followed them like a shadow, even in a friendly country. We have heard allegations of harassment of women by security forces at the water collection points, and regular sexual abuse of refugee women by the security forces has also been reported. It is not easy to address these problems in a situation when all the camp officials are men and they work entirely through the — mostly male — Mahjhis.

Recognising gender issues

There was no specific gender component in our initial water programme but gradually we started responding to the gender issues. It is difficult to work in a gender-blind situation, where every decision is taken and implemented by male officials living in the bachelors' dormitory far from their family, with no positive motivation to work with distressed people. As the only organisation whose staff live in the camp, we have some advantages over other organisations whose workers are only available during the day. Moreover, from the very beginning, we tried to stick to the principle of 'more female, less male' in the working team. Female engineers and health educators became our strength in pointing out and responding to women's concerns. Moving the tap-stands to a safer location, to avoid harassment of women by a section of the security forces, and changing the timing of supplying water to suit the routines of both the women and the men was the first attempt to change the gender-blind situation into a positive gender-sensitive approach.

Refugees queueing for water at the tapstand provided by Oxfam.   Howard Davies/Oxfam

Setting up women's health centres

Health educators tried to make it possible for the women to benefit from the services and health education programme by arranging women's gatherings and group meetings. Later on this became difficult, when camp officials banned all group meetings and gatherings to prevent any anti-repatriation activity. Then the team took new initiatives to reach the women by setting up women's centres in the camp. In the first phase the women's centres, which were called 'health education centres' to make them more acceptable, were constructed by a mixture of voluntary and paid labour. Later on we supplied the materials and women managed the construction on their own. Gradually these centres became a refuge for the women, a place of talking, sharing of emotions and releasing of tensions. Health educators also benefited from these centres as a place of contact and discussion.

Refugee women proposed to use the centre for their children as children's health education centres (schools were not allowed), in the morning while the women were busy with cooking and other domestic activities. That gave birth to our 'child to child' programme.

Ultimately these centres became the learning place for the health educators as well. New ideas for garbage disposal, construction of women's bathing places using refugee voluntary labour, ways of using the refugee labour in desludging full latrines, watching the water sources, guarding and protecting the latrines and other communal areas, all came up from the discussions at the women's centres. The original idea behind these centres was just to make better contact with families, and hence the refugee community at large, through the women and children; but gradually they became more than that. Individuals who are attending the centres are also getting benefits personally. The benefits are often intangible — some comfort or ease, perhaps, from the informally organised activities in congenial company.

Attempts to close the health education centres

When the health education centres became the women's centres in a real sense, the male folk, both officials and refugees, felt threatened and started plotting a conspiracy against them. It has become a common practice of chief camp officials to issue verbal orders to our health educators and sometimes to our coordinator to close down the centres, claiming that they are the breeding ground of conspiracy against repatriation, and other anti-law-and-order activities. This has never been backed up with evidence, and we continue. A desperate and very organised attempt was made in the last 'Ramadan' (the Muslim holy fasting month), when a group of male Mahjhi sought permission to convert a centre into a mosque (where women's entrance is not encouraged). The women resisted from the very beginning when they heard about it. Giving up the attempt, the Mahjhis changed their strategy and sought permission for using the centres just for one month. Again, it was the women of the centres who uncovered the plot. They warned the health educators about the consequences of the proposal if we endorsed it. 'We will never be able to change the status of a mosque into a women's centre no matter what the agreement was.' This is how a mere sitting and chatting place of women become a source of power and learning for both parties.

Protecting the rights of women refugees

It is true that as refugee workers with the limited responsibility of supplying water and ensuring sanitation we have very little scope to play a substantial role to protect women like Amina or to allow them repatriation with dignity, but I don't think we should not try. If we can organise the refugees, especially the refugee women, through women volunteers and workers and achieve some confidence among them I think nothing is impossible.

If we can organise the refugees, especially the refugee women, ... I think nothing is impossible.

It is also high time to detail the requirements to protect women's rights in refugee camp situations, on behalf of NGOs who are willing to be involved in future refugee programmes managed by UNHCR in a situation where local authorities have different attitudes and conceptions. Otherwise NGOs will remain the enlisted or pre-qualified subcontractors of UNHCR, with no choice. Nobody will be there to ensure UNHCR actually achieves its own intention of ensuring gender issues are addressed in a positive way in every programme.

Gawher Nayeem Wahra is a Disasters Officer with Oxfam Bangladesh and responsible for work on emergencies and disaster-preparedness.

Saharawi women: 'between ambition and suffering'

Tina Wallace

The title is a quotation from a paper written by G'nah Allah Ayat, a woman doctor who is a Saharawi refugee working with Saharawis in the refugee camps of Algeria. The paper was presented at a conference on Saharawi women refugees organised in the House of Commons by One World Action, on 28 October 1993. The conference raised a number of critical issues concerning Saharawi women and their experience as long-term refugees in camps, and also more widely about women refugees and how women learn to cope with the suffering that emergencies such as war and famine impose on them. It was both a moving occasion, when the hardships and pain experienced by these women were powerfully expressed, and an inspiring one, where the strength and innovation of these women were graphically presented.

The conference was opened by Glenys Kinnock, chair of One World Action, who made a number of points about women refugees and how women cope with such displacement all over the world. She stressed the need to look at the rights, demands, and challenges of refugee women, especially Saharawi women. In order to do this, however, there are a number of barriers to be overcome. First, the stereotyping of refugee women, especially in Africa, that is becoming more and more prevalent in the Western media,

and in the advertisements of many aid agencies. All the work done on the importance of images seems not to have modified old stereotypes, and she stressed that women refugees are almost always portrayed negatively, as anguished women, helpless, needing to be 'saved'. While it is true that refugee women are experiencing loss, and often destitution, it is also true that in order to survive they have to help themselves. They could not survive solely on the basis of waiting for outside help — which often never comes. Many women suffering in the aftermath of emergencies actually lead the fight for survival.

Second, in order to get a fuller and truer picture of the realities of life for refugee women, they must receive our attention. Only when we stop to listen and talk to them can we hear about their fight for the future, their abilities to change and create new structures and ways of working in alien environments. The papers delivered by the Saharawi women refugees themselves highlighted the impressive work they have undertaken, in health, education and agriculture, for example.

Third, it is important to look at the rights of refugees, women and men, and address the problems that deny them their rights; it is necessary to confront the causes of their situation. This conference highlighted the range of rights that

Saharawi women are demanding: access to health and education; political and economic recognition; full and equal participation in society.

Lastly Glenys Kinnock pointed out that it is essential to support women in their transition back to peace and a return home. In many emergency situations women play new roles previously undertaken by men; they also take on many new and wide-ranging family and community responsibilities, and in so doing widen their horizons. However, the experience of women throughout this century has shown that when hostilities cease, during the 'return to normality', many of these roles and responsibilities, new rights and freedoms are taken away from them, and they are forced back into subsidiary roles and secondary status.

Women's empowerment

The issue of the particular oppression women often suffer as refugees, through gender-related persecution, sexual harassment, and gender-blind procedures, was raised in a paper by Georgina Ashworth looking at the plight of refugee women worldwide. But the Saharawi women stressed that they themselves have not experienced this kind of sexual oppression in the camps. They have managed to avoid this by maintaining a social cohesion through upholding social traditions and customs, and they have controlled the day-to-day running of the camps.

One of the major achievements for Saharawi women has been their empowerment within the context of camp life, and the development of women leaders in many fields. During their time in the camps they have built up an impressive schooling system for girls as well as boys, and run literacy classes for the whole camp population. Many women have themselves undergone skills training and now are

Women took responsibility for much of the administration of the camps, including food distribution
ANDREW RUTHERFORD/ONE WORLD ACTION

teachers, nurses, and clerical assistants within the camps. A few have gone on to achieve higher levels of education and become doctors, for example, but the women stressed the fact that in order to continue education beyond secondary level it is necessary to leave the camps, and access to places and scholarships abroad are far less available to women than men. This is an experience encountered by all women refugees, who find the gender bias in education provision for refugees in Europe severely discriminates against them. (See, for example, 'It ain't half sexist Mum', Jane Goldsmith, World University Service, London 1987).

Saharawi women found that they had to take on the running of the camps because the men were absent, and they have risen to the challenge and become managers — running schools, clinics, agricultural

Livestock-rearing was one of the many projects set up by women refugees.

projects and neighbourhood committees. This area of management was an entirely new area for women.

Women have become involved in every aspect of life, and taken responsibility in all major areas. This has not been done easily, there has been a huge cost in physical and emotional terms: 'The multi-faceted nature of women's work; in the tents, in the local administration and small-holdings, in the bakeries, workshops, clinics and meetings, is arduous and tedious. Such hard work requires immense physical and moral effort which perhaps would be easier to bear for women working in better conditions with more resources and improved professional training.' (Ayat) They have been largely self-taught and had to learn from experience.

Responsibilities and social organisation

No-one should underestimate the hardships and constraints experienced by these women. Their husbands and fathers are away or dead, families are broken up and scattered because of war, children may be dispersed in order to find higher education outside the camps. These women have to run their homes, maintain the norms of traditional hospitality, care for their children, and combine these domestic tasks with fuel and water collection, difficult in such a hard environment. In addition many of them undertake new roles and responsibilities outside the home. All this work is undertaken in a desert setting which is bleak (except for the innovative and successful agricultural projects they have set up) and extremely cold in winter and very hot in summer.

These women have survived by organising: their lives, the distribution of aid, work, and responsibility. They have organised in such a way as to include everyone, to ensure no-one feels marginalised or excluded. This has built up social cohesiveness, in a context where conditions could so easily have fragmented the entire community.

Looking to the future

Now the thoughts of Saharawi women are turning to the future, to a time when the crisis will end and they can start a new life. They have been watching and learning from the experience of other women involved in conflict and emergencies. They have seen a pattern repeated where, after the return home, men and the constitution or legal system have withdrawn the new rights, roles and responsibilities from women. The Saharawi women want to hold on to the gains they have made during the last painful years, and to combine their roles within the home and outside the home as teachers, nurses, administrators, managers and participants in daily political life in a way which is beneficial to them and to the whole society.

The importance of having a good legal framework, and a constitution which enshrines the rights of women, was discussed as part of a presentation by an international lawyer, Christine Chinkin. While she acknowledged the failure of international and national laws to protect women in many cases, she nevertheless stressed the need for a good legal framework at all levels within which women could argue and press for their rights. Saharawi women want to play a key part in writing the new constitution when hostilities cease.

Reality, not stereotypes

The presentations at the conference belied the stereotypes and passive images of refugee women so prevalent today in the North. These women were not passive victims, mere recipients of outside aid, helpless, powerless. Far from it. The over-riding lesson of the day was one which we have learned before, but keep forgetting!

That is that when we listen to refugee women from around the world we hear again and again these realities — that they have to depend on themselves for survival, they have to shoulder the responsibility for family and community, they have to find ways to provide health care, education, food, shelter, water. They are the ones that have to organise, provide, nurture and fight for a future for themselves and their families.

The importance of giving space to these women to tell their story, and for others to listen, cannot be over-emphasised. Similarly, the need for aid agencies to tell this story rather than reproduce tired and misleading pictures and reports of refugee women cannot be stressed enough. Their fight deserves every encouragement, their voices must be heard if the right kind of support is to be given, and their rights must be respected. It is only by listening to and learning from these women that people and agencies in the North can understand what is required and how to target their money and communications work in a way which will be relevant and effective.

References

G'nah Allah Ayat, 'Saharawi women: between ambition and suffering'. Paper presented at One World Action Conference, London, 1993.

Jane Goldsmith, 'It ain't half sexist Mum', World University Service, London. 1987.

A full report of the conference *Today's Refugees: Tomorrow's Leaders* is available from One World Action, Floor 5, Weddel House, 13–14 West Smithfield, London EC 1A 9HY, at a cost of £4 plus 50p post and packing.

Tina Wallace is Co-ordinator of the Strategic Planning and Evaluation Team in Oxfam.

Oxfam is grateful to One World Action for supplying the photographs used in this paper.

INTERVIEW

Krishnamurthy Pushpanath

The Zambian experience of drought in 1992/3 was notable for the collaboration between government and non-governmental organisations in the relief interventions. Krishnamurthy Pushpanath, who was Oxfam's Regional Representative for Malawi and Zambia from 1988 to 1993, describes here how relief programmes were designed with community participation and with a view to the implications for long-term development.

The drought in Zambia in 1991/92 — it was historic. In 50 years the people of Zambia and Southern Africa had not faced a disaster of such intensity, extent and magnitude. So we were dealing with a community of people with no memory, no experience of facing such a crisis. We needed to be clear that our approach to drought should not lead to handouts; we didn't want to make beggars out of people but recognise their innate potential and ability to work in a way that means they control what they do, they have a say, and it gives them an opportunity to practise what we mean by 'the grass-roots democratic process' — because a new politics was ushered in in Zambia just before that.

How did you involve everyone?
We had been working with groups of women, groups of men, youth, and so on over a period of time. So we had already made a breakthrough, in terms of linking ourselves up. With the civil servants as well: in 1989 we had held a disaster workshop at national level. So we had some key people — they were our catalytic agents in those districts, and we could get

reasonably accurate information. As to the feedback from the people — men and women were different, obviously. Men, for instance, would look at immediately having some food to be given free. But the women would be saying 'no, let's do something about the water', because in some villages women used to wake up at 2.00 a.m. and literally scoop water from the well. Women would say, too, that they needed to be involved in whatever we were doing. In Eastern Province about 35-40 per cent of the population are female-headed households, for historic reasons. So you have different views. We were aware that there were going to be different views and we were looking out for it. Because of our long-term relationship it was easy. People might think that if you talk to women then you wouldn't be able to get to the bottom of what the story is. But because we were experiencing the process of — if you like — social analysis of the area, we were able to get to that.

Moving from assessment to the actual programme, how did what you had learnt in the assessment shape the programme?
Immediately after that assessment we

asked people to identify two traditional authority areas in each District which had already run out of food, or which were going to run out of food. In these two areas we would have a mass workshop. We would inform people 24 hours beforehand and organise them through our catalytic agents, the civil servants. We used a public address system and had a workshop under the sky, at which there were anywhere between 500 and 5,000 people. We would brainstorm with them, on what did they identify as the problem? How did they rank this problem? What did they want to do about it? It was clear to them that Oxfam had come to help, so that perception and expectations were bound to be there. But we wanted to be honest and transparent about what we could do and what they could do. That was the process which we used to identify the crucial issues, what to do about them, and who was going to do it.

Key people in each traditional area were elected, in an open election. We made sure, and one of our women colleagues, Nawina, was also making sure, that one of the conditions was that at least 50 per cent of the people elected should be women. The women were quite happy. For the first time some of them held a public address system in their hands, and it was a really exciting process. Men would laugh at this, and say 'No, they can't do this' but they saw that once the women got going they were actually communicating. They could also see that we were listening to them. And men are pretty careful in this kind of situation; they know there is a crisis and that if they try and shut up their women probably, this so-called giver might not give. They were also able to see that. So that's how it happened; and we set up the Village Community Committees — the Receiving Committee, Distribution Committee, Monitoring Committee and Accounting Committee — each one linked up to District level.

How well did these structures work?
In some places, very effectively. It was the first time those people were being given an opportunity where they could do, think, plan, decide, and execute. They realised they could actually question people, that the relief was coming in their name. It was effective from the village level committees up to the chief level committees. In other cases we found that it was a mixed experience, the committees were misused, there was some abuse, centralisation of power, men dominating women; in some cases, women dominating the rest.

The most interesting part in Eastern Province is 'the Oxfam women' — that was what they were called. They were small groups, five or six groups of ten to 15 women, and they would stand up to anybody. In one area they did the whole organisation for the meeting as well. In that way they were able to articulate for the rest of the people. That's when we found out our development work with these women's groups had not just given them an opportunity to grow more food, but an opportunity to gain insight into their problems, to gain self-confidence, and to articulate that in public and really take on anybody. So these women were, if you like, the vanguard leaders of the moment. Generally these committees, at least to the extent of the short-term objective for which they were set up, did far better than we had anticipated.

What happened after the drought, once the immediate crisis was over? Has the momentum continued? What has happened in the recovery period?
Even in the relief phase we were looking at agriculture, because the main livelihood for most people is agriculture or forest resources. We had already recognised that the 30-40 per cent of peasant families — most of them female-headed households — suffer in not being able to produce enough food at the household level. Most families

Grain store being built as part of the drought–recovery programme.   BAZ SOLANKI/OXFAM

were producing only enough food for four to six months, mainly because these women have serious labour constraints. At the time of sowing and ploughing they're moving around, scrounging for food, and working on somebody else's land. So they work very little land and produce very little. Good seed, consequently, is a problem for them, and they do not have even basic tools. Most of the agriculture of the peasant household is done manually. In our first assessment we found that there were hardly any tools, so we were able to provide those, and proper seed, provided in time: and they had relief food. We also looked at the culture. There was an existing practice of people working together; they would brew beer for a group to come and work together. We suggested they collect their own group, a group of five women, or a group of women and men of different ages, to work together in each person's plot in a cyclical way, and use the food provided. So now they had labour, they pooled their tools, they had good seeds, and they were able to extend their land as

well. For the first time these women, who had not previously had enough food, had more food than they had ever grown. We identified some families which in two generations had never grown as much food as they grew this particular season. Never!

I don't mean that it was all fantastically successful. There were problems, seed was late, or got poorly distributed; in some cases they ate the seed because the maize did not come for food consumption during the relief time. But by and large the result of the relief agriculture programme, which was regarded as both a recovery and development intervention, led to substantial production — 70,000 households were covered, 70 per cent of them were women, and 70 per cent of that 70 per cent were female-headed households. It was an amazing achievement. We were able to identify clearly what the problems were, who was being hurt by the problems — in this case women — and give them the opportunity to stand up and show leadership.

We were able to mobilise women, and

some of them did an extraordinary job. Some of the people who emerged were called 'the new leaders' in their villages but, having created the potential for women to come forward and participate, our back-up support for them was not sufficiently thought through. This was a failure on our part. Once you mobilise women you should provide support systems, which can't be the same as for men's groups. I think we misfired there, and in the process there were a lot of women leaders who dropped out. It was not their fault, we were not able to give them sufficient back-up. Without that, you make the women more vulnerable and they will lose the kind of social protection they had — good, bad, or ugly. There is a danger there.

What kind of back-up do you think you can give? Does it mean working with the men as well?

Yes. Interestingly, this is the first time in Eastern Province that we have worked a lot with men. Otherwise our work has been largely with women. And in the process men have also changed a lot. They have said, 'Our women can do more things than we thought they could.' And it is true among civil servants as well, who were volunteers in the district. For the first time women had the opportunity to take on a leadership role at the district level and even those civil servants — men, and women themselves — have said they got more confidence.

What more can be done? We need sufficient programme people, both men and women, we need to make more frequent visits, and we need to have different kinds of meetings at a time which is suitable for women. You have to find out the time when they are free, and make provision for taking care of the children, and so on. In that way we would have found out what the problems were, why they were dropping out, what our

intervention should be. This might be more intensive, it might involve more cost, but it might also involve a different approach to them; and it would also involve getting the men to support them. It has happened to some extent by itself but I think that is what we should be doing.

Quite often when an initial crisis has passed or, for instance, a war is over, the gains that women seem to have made, disappear, and they slip back into what they were doing previously. Do you think this is likely to happen in the aftermath of the drought?

That is an interesting question. Disaster gives an enormous opportunity. The mindset of individuals and communities is very different. They are prepared to experiment with long-established practice and tradition. Once that happens our intervention should make the most of that opportunity. Because of the crisis, people were able to experiment, they allowed women to participate, and so on. That happened, it is a living example. We have to quickly get in there. That is what our recovery programme is all about. We are working in just two districts now, but we feel that in these two districts we might be able to back up the leadership which emerged. Because the area is much smaller we will be able to work more intensively with them.

We have planned some training in their own villages, and we are trying out some of the women, who have just been to third form or fourth form at school, as researchers, gathering information, preparing family profiles, and looking at what is the endowment, or the entitlement, of the family. This is being done by ordinary village people, with no formal training at all, and it is making them feel far more powerful. They are able to analyse information. We don't ask the question 'Who are the poor?' but 'Who are the rich?' You find again and again that hardly any women are seen as rich. We ask why that is. I feel optimistic that we will continue not only to strengthen women but also to sensitise men who are working with women at committee level, in addressing livelihoods problems, which include household food security.

Oxfam is just one actor on the scene. What is happening at the official level? How is that relating to the recognition of women's abilities and women's needs?

This drought gave us an opportunity to look at underlying causes. You can have failure of rain and no crop but still people can be quite happy. A disaster only happens when it affects people. In the Zambian case the implementation of structural adjustment exacerbated an already existing problem of women having no access, no resources, and so on. The drought came as the last straw. We were able to use this experience. The most important aspect of this drought intervention was continuous and consistent communication of what was happening, why it was happening, what was being done about it — in the local media, lobbying with the bilaterals, lobbying the multi-laterals, getting out information. Now, when the World Bank is looking at Zambia as a whole, they have organised a workshop on Engendering Development. We were able to highlight those issues and I think it only happened because of that disaster and the opportunity that we had.

I don't mean to say that everything is going to be wonderful now because we communicated these messages, but I think for the first time everybody is really thinking that they need to address the gender issue: how men and women are affected differently,what the policies should be, and the resource commitment. Those are the debates that are emerging now, which I think is pretty positive.

Is this debate taking place at government level and within the government structures?

Very much so. At government level, at civil servant level, at village level. You have these micro experiences linking up at macro level. Everybody says 'we have a problem, can you give us a solution?' The solution should be to start with a clear political commitment. Once you have a political commitment you start following that up with policies, once you have the policies you have the resources. If you really want to address the gender issue it requires a number of things: the institutional mechanism to address the problem, the government policies, and the resources. It is going to be an uphill, long-drawn-out task, and will often be reversible; but I think there is far more openness now to see the reality of the problems, and I think this experience has helped us to arrive at that situation.

The more intensely you work, the more rigorous you are, the more you try to find out what are the fundamental causes that affect and impoverish families, men and women together, you start to understand how little you know. That is the premise on which we should be working, not on the kind of arrogant feeling that we already know all that. We have seen more and more clearly the complexities of the relationship. There are cultural practices which are gender-positive. We need to be able to detect those and support them. At the same time we should be able to find out those cultural practices which are gender-negative towards women. My view is that we need to be humble enough to be far more experimental with ourselves, not with the community, in terms of finding out and allowing people to have their say. We should accept we will make mistakes, but in good faith; and that will only lead us to greater understanding.

Resources

Book review

If women ruled the world, there would be less war ... Perhaps that is too simple, but if 'feminine' values gained more place in politics, violence would lose its respectability as a way of resolving conflict, to be replaced by reconciliation, compromise and other non-violent methods. Whether such approaches to conflict resolution are biological or culturally-determined characteristics of women is a question Jeanne Vickers does not go into. The urgent and practical point is that non-violent approaches have to be elevated to greater status and effectiveness in the male-dominated world of political power.

Women and War urges women to recognise the powers that they have, and to use them to reduce the incidence of war. Women should 'think global' about the devastation war causes, and 'act local' to demand non-war options wherever possible. As well as a four-page bibliography, the book includes outline plans for seminars and discussions to help readers raise awareness in their own communities.

The end of the Cold War did not bring the hoped-for 'peace dividend'. We now have more wars, more deaths (especially civilian deaths), and a higher level of arms expenditure. Among the causes of war, Vickers names the arms trade, bad diplomacy, and value systems which elevate power and patriotic nationalism at the expense of less aggressive values such as respect for individuals, or quality of life.

Why should women in particular be trying to combat war? Because it is women who suffer most heavily from its direct and indirect impacts. Militarism reinforces for the inequalities and violence against women prevalent in most societies. It also diverts resources from development, and it is women who suffer most from lack of health services, poor education, and sluggish economies, not least because they form the largest proportion of the poor everywhere. Equality for women and peace go hand in hand: women must realise this, and combine women's and peace movements to form a doubly powerful force for change.

Vickers reviews the achievements of the UN Decade for Women, and quotes substantially from the 'Forward-looking Strategies' agreed at the end of the decade, as well as statements from international women's movements. Like so many international ideals these are still only paper commitments. Vickers calls for women to join together to demand obedience to them, from their governments, industries, local communities and themselves.

The cost of covering such an enormous subject in a slim book is, inevitably, superficiality. Sometimes this does not matter: readers may be content to take on trust that 'women and children are the principal victims of war'. But there are also problematic political questions which Vickers takes for granted, such as whether it is the nature of leaders or the nature of states themselves that is confrontational and war-like; and whether a strengthened and interventionist UN is really a sure and simple prescription for reducing war

The book is somewhat Northern-centred. Arms production is highlighted as a major cause of war, and many of the women peace activists held up as models are anti-nuclear protestors, or — as examples of those who realise the essential links between feminist and peace demands — women who worked against the First World War. Little space is given to the roles of women in preventing violent conflicts in the South, where the social dynamics, politics and economics of war may be very different.

However, the essential message is relevant to all women. The world should not continue to suffer its current level of militarism; under pressure and example from women, the dominant (masculine) culture which produces this militarism must change. Men have to become more humanely responsible for their societies, more ready to forego their own ambitions and seek conciliation, less apt to resort to violence. Women have many roles to play in bringing about this change. One contribution they can make is in education for peace — including education in gender roles. This is something that women can and should be working for in different ways everywhere.

Review by Kitty Warnock, Co-ordinator, Women and Conflict Project, PANOS.

Women and War is written by Jeanne Vickers and published in 1993 by Zed Press, London. ISBN 1 85649 230 3

Further reading

African Rights (1993) *The nightmare continues ... Abuses against Somali refugees in Kenya.*

Anderson, M B and Woodrow, P (1989) *Rising from the Ashes: Development Strategies in Times of Disaster*, Westview Press, Boulder.

Arnaout, G (1987) *Guidelines setting out the objectives for the international protection of refugee women and girls and possible means of achieving them*, UNHCR, Geneva.

Augsburger, D W (1992) *Conflict Mediation across Cultures*, Westminster/John Knox Press, Louisville, Kentucky.

Brazeau, A (1990) *Gender sensitive development planning in the refugee context*. Paper presented to the Expert Group on Refugee and Disabled and Displaced Women and Children, UNHCR, Geneva.

Buchanan-Smith, M (1993) *The Entitlement System: A Review of Oxfam's Approach to Relief Food Distribution in Samburu and Turkana Districts of Kanya 1992/3*, IDS, Brighton.

Cuny F C (1983) *Disasters and Development*, New York: Oxford University Press.

Drew, L (1991) 'Don't forget the children', *Emergency Preparedness Digest* 18(4):10-11.

Drolet, P (M B Anderson, ed) (1991) *Vocational Skills Training for Refugees: A Case Study*, Collaborative for Development Action, Inc.

Dupree, N H (1991) *Observations on Afghan women refugees in Pakistan: 1990*, World Refugee Survey.

Ferris, E G (1993) *Beyond Borders: Refugees, Migrants and Human Rights in the Post-Cold-War Era*, WCC Publications, Geneva.

Hall, E (1988) *Vocational Training for Women Refugees in Africa: Guidelines from Selected Field Projects*, Training Policies, Paper #26, Geneva: ILO.

Hancock, K (1988) *Refugee Women and Children in Somalia: Their Social and Psychological Needs*, Mogadischu: UNICEF.

Hiegel J P (1984) 'Collaboration with traditional healers: experience in refugees' mental care', *International Journal of Mental Health* 12(3).

Horn of Africa Project War and Famine (1988). *Indigenous Perspectives on Conflict in the Horn of Africa*, Institute of Peace and Conflict Studies. Waterloo, Canada: Conrad Grebel College.

Kennedy, B (1992) 'The effects of famine on women with special reference to Africa', *Focus*, Issue 46, Dublin, Ireland.

Kibreab, G (1987) *Refugees and Development in Africa: The Case of Eritrea*, Trenton, New Jersey: The Red Sea Press.

Kinyanjui, K (1991) *Refugees in Africa: in search of hope,* IDRC Reports (19(3):4-6.

McCallin, M (1991) 'The convention on the rights of the child: an instrument to address the psychosocial needs of refugee children', *International Journal of Refugee Law* 3(1):82-89.

McCallin, M, and Fozzard S (1990) *The Impact of Traumatic Events on the Psychological Well-Being of Mozambican Refugee Women and Children,* Geneva: ICCB.

Mears, C and Chowdhury, S, *Health Care for Refugees and Displaced People,* Oxfam Practical Health Guide 9, Oxfam (forthcoming).

Merriman, P A and Browitt, C W A (eds) (1993) *Natural disasters: protecting vulnerable communities,* Thomas Telford, London.

Migration News 2:1 (1992) *Uprooted children.*

Muller, M (1988) 'Increasing the effectiveness of a latrines programme', *World Health Forum* 9.

Moser, C O N (1993) *Gender Planning and Development: Theory, Practice and Training,* Routledge, London and New York.

Myers, D G (1989) 'Mental health and disaster', In *Psychosocial Aspects of Disaster,* R Gist and B Lubin (eds) New York: John Wiley & Sons.

O'Keefe, P, et al (1976) 'Taking the naturalness out of natural disasters', *Nature* 260:566-67.

Organizacion Panamericana de la Salud OPS/OMS (1990) *Reunion Centroamericana el Papel de la Mujer en los Preparativos para Desastres y los Socorros,* San Jose, Costa Rica.

Parente, P (1989) 'Women and emergency settlements', *Proceedings of Settlements and Disasters,* DERC. Delft University.

Rais de Lerner, G, and Tapia de Peralta I (1981). *La Mujer Latinoamericana y La Migracion Forzada,* Caracas: Programa de Atencion Psico-Social. Servicio Social Internacional, Comision Venozolana.

Rangasami, A(1985) *Women's Roles and Strategies During Food Crises and Famines,* Fell, Paris.

Reddy, G (1992) *Women foragers: survival strategies of poor women under drought and scarcity in a semi-arid region,* Conference on Population Movements, Food Crises and Community Response, Department of Social Anthropology, S V University, Tirupati, India.

Ressler, E M N Boothby, and D J Steinbock (1988). *Unaccompanied Children: Care and Placement in Wars, Natural Disasters and Refugee Movements,* New York: OUP.

Rivers, J P W (1982) 'Women and children last: an essay on sex discrimination in disasters', *Disasters* 6(4):256-267.

Sanday, P (1974) 'Female status in the public domain', In *Woman, Culture and Society,* M Z Rosaldo and L Lamphere, (eds), Stanford: Stanford University Press.

Sen, A (1981) 'Ingredients of famine analysis: availability and entitlements', *The Quarterly Journal of Economics* :432-464.

Spring, A (1982) 'Women and men as refugees: differential assimilation of Angolan refugees in Zambia', In *Involuntary Migration and Resettlement: The Problems and Responses of Dislocated People,* A Hansen and A Oliver-Smith, (eds), Boulder: Westview Press.

Stark, S (1989) *Report on the Situation of Women and Children in UN and UNHCR Administered Refugee Operations,* Women's Commission for Refugee Women and Children, New York, USA.

Staunton, I (ed) (1990) *Mothers of the Revolution,* Harare: Baobab Books.

Stoltenberg, K (1991) *Working with Women in Emergency Relief and Rehabilitation Programmes,* League of Red Cross and Red Crescent Societies, Geneva.

UNDP (1990) *Refugee and Displaced Women in Africa.* UNECA. Arusha.

UNDRO NEWS (1991) *Women and Disaster Management,* July/August. Based on "The Role of Women NNAs is Disaster Management", *International Nursing Review,* Nov/Dec 1990.

UNESCO, *Annual Summary of Information on Natural Disasters,* Geneva.

UN (1990) *UNHCR Policy on Refugee Women,* A/AC.96/754 (20 August 1990), Geneva.

UNHCR (1988) *Guidelines on Refugee Children,* UNHCR (August 1988).

UNHCR (1991a) *Sectoral Checklists for Refugee Women and Children,* Geneva.

UNHCR (1991b) *Guidelines on the Protection of Refugee Women,* Geneva.

UNHCR (1991c) *Progress Report on the Implementation of the UNHCR Policy on Refugee Women,* EC/SC.2/47, Geneva.

UNHCR and Refugee Policy Group (1985) *A Selected and Annotated Bibliography on Refugee Women,* Geneva.

Vickers, J (1993) *Women and War,* Zed Books, London.

Wilson, K (1992) 'Assisting the most vulnerable refugees', *Refugee Participation Network* 12

Wiest, R (1992) *The Needs of Women and Children in Disasters and Emergencies,* University of Manitoba Disaster Research Unit, Winnipeg.

Wingo, G (1990) *Changes in Female Attitudes and Social Well-Being; Preparing for Repatriation: A Pilot Study in Two Afghan Refugee Villages in Baluchistan,* UNHCR Sub Office, Quetta: Radda Barnen/Swedish Save the Children. .

Young, H (1992) *Food Scarcity and Famine, Assessment and Response,* Oxfam Practical Health Guide No 7, Oxfam.

News from GADU

Forward to Beijing

The Conference itself

The Fourth UN World Conference on Women, will be held between 4 and 15 September, 1995, in Beijing, China. Governments will review the ways in which they have implemented the Forward Looking Strategies (FLS) adopted at the Third World Conference in Nairobi in 1985 which outlined the commitments of governments to work towards equality, development and peace for women. The Conference will review and appraise progress since 1985 and will adopt a Plan of Action to remove obstacles to the advancement of women.

The NGO Forum

The NGO international Forum will also be held in Beijing, between 30 August and 12 September. This is an open gathering, when hundreds of workshops are organised on any theme by any group who can get themselves there and bring an audience together. It offers women the opportunity to find out about existing research, initiate new research, open consultation with governments, and to build coalitions.

NAWO

On behalf of the UK National Alliance of Women's Organisations (NAWO), Oxfam is collating an NGO report for the UK Overseas Development Administration. As part of the preparations for Beijing, ODA is working on a report to measure changes in the status of women in relation to men, and any progress in implementing the FLS since 1985.

The Women's Linking Project

The review of programme work on gender for the Women's Linking Project provides an opportunity for Oxfam to measure progress made towards equality, development and peace for women, as indicators from the FLS have been integrated into the review guidelines. Case studies will provide information on the main issues for women in the future.

The work of field offices

Two project officers from Oxfam India attended a meeting in Delhi to find out what was happening at their national level. An inter-agency facilitating committee for Beijing (IFCB-India) has been formed to ensure effective NGO participation in the preparatory process and the Conference. A decentralised system of 25 field-level institutions will disseminate information, organise meetings, and elicit feedback from grassroots women and groups on issues affecting the lives of women in general and poor women in particular. Mallika Singh, coordinator of the Oxfam gender network for Oxfam in Asia (AGRA), is delighted with the opportunities offered by the Beijing conference. She says 'it was difficult to put the thrill and excitement of what is happening on paper!'

Oxfam gender policy

On 13 May 1993 Oxfam Council of Trustees ratified an organisation-wide gender policy, and plans are now being drawn up for implementation. The principles of the policy emphasise Oxfam's focus on gender rather than women, to ensure that improving women's status is the responsibility of both sexes. Oxfam is committed to improving the lives of women through its development and relief programmes, by promoting women's access to basic needs, education, skills, and decision-making, and supporting women's organisations. Oxfam is also committed to integrating a gender perspective into communications and advocacy work. Copies of the policy are available from GADU.

ODA gender workshop

Daniel McCallum, of Oxfam's Cofunding team, attended an ODA/NGO workshop on gender and development at the University of Edinburgh 5-7 July 1993. One objective was to find ways of integrating gender into both project planning and the policies and strategies of organisations by providing a forum for networking among NGOs, ODA staff, and consultants. A questionnaire will be circulated in six months' time on actions taken and changes brought about as a result of the workshop.

International conference on population and development (ICPD)

Women played a significant role in the second PrepCom (Preparatory Committee) for the ICPD, in New York in May 1993. Claudia Garcia-Moreno, Health Unit Coordinator, attended as one of the NGO representatives in the UK official delegation. Women were able to influence the wording and structure of official documents in the conference process and, as in the UN Conference on Human Rights in June 1993, the Women's Caucus was successful in finding a language that was women-centred.

Integrating gender into official documents

Making changes to the wording of official documents is an important first stage for integrating a gender perspective into the population and development concerns, particularly the new 'World Population Plan of Action'. Two important changes were the chapter on 'the role and status of women' becoming 'the empowerment of women and gender equality', and the chapter on 'family planning' being retitled 'reproductive rights, reproductive health and family planning'.

The Women's Caucus

The Caucus met every morning to share views and information, and enabled women on official delegations to be fully briefed on the concerns of women in NGOs. Women have learned from experience at previous UN meetings — successful lobbying allowed space for NGOs in the official proceedings, uncommon at UN meetings.

Women's concerns

In the population debate women emphasise the need for a wider understanding of the issues, that will benefit women in a more holistic way which allows them more control over their lives. The focus should be on reproductive rights and reproductive health, rather than only on family planning. Reproductive health services should provide such things

512106

as sex education, (treatment of sexually access to safe abortion services, and safe pregnancy and delivery. There should be greater emphasis on male responsibility for sexuality, fertility, and child-rearing. Traditional concepts of the family often do not guarantee the reproductive rights of individuals. The increased emphasis on the threat of population growth and international migration is preventing a full consideration of consumption patterns as part of the link between population and environmental problems.

Country processes

Lobbying of UN processes by women is essential, but it is at national level that words can be translated into action. Women can work with NGOs to press for government policies that improve people's lives.

What next?

Work on official documentation continues; the Secretariat willsubmit an annotated outline to the next UN General Assembly. There will be a draft document by February 1994, which will form the basis of discussion at PrepCom 3, 4-22 April 1993, in New York, to which any NGO with UN consultative status can send suggestions.

If you would like further information about ICPD or would like to circulate *Women's Voices*, the Southern NGO statement to all participants in the ICPD process, write to Carmen Diaz Olivo, International Women's Health Coalition, 24 East 21st Street, 5th floor, New York NY 10010 fax: (212) 979 9009. If you would like a copy of Oxfam's position paper on population and reproductive rights and planning, contact us in GADU, OXFAM, 274 Banbury Road, Oxford OX2 7DZ, UK, phone: (865) 312363 or fax (865) 312600.

rence on uprooted ...m women

Misconceptions and misinformation about Islam have a negative impact on the provision of appropriate resources for Muslim refugee women. Listening to them, learning about their experiences, and making recommendations to Western humanitarian organisations working on their behalf is the aim of an international conference on uprooted Muslim women, to be held in the United Arab Emirates, 11-14 September 1994, organised by the International Working Group on Refugee Women.

Current refugee situations involving Muslim women are many and varied: Afghanistan, Somalia, and Bosnia illustrate the diversity of cultural backgrounds. Different countries and communities interpret the Qu'ran and Sharia law in different ways, which affect the position of women. Organisations working with refugees need to look more closely at particular cultural conditions, in order to develop appropriate responses. The conference brings together refugee and displaced women, researchers, policy makers and practitioners involved in refugee assistance.

Themes for plenary sessions and workshops include values and perceptions in Islam and the Islamic law of conduct, effective strategies for mobilising women to self-reliance, third country adjustment, and mobilising funds. It is hoped that a handbook based on the workshops will be published, to provide a practical guide to working with uprooted Muslim women.

For further details, contact Marie-France Belay, c/o Webster University, 13-15 route de Collex, CH1293 Bellevue, Geneva, Switzerland. Tel: (22) 774 452, fax: (22) 774 3013.